# THE BRAVEST TEENAGE YANKS

# The Bravest Teenage Yanks

by

WILLARD A. HEAPS

DUELL, SLOAN AND PEARCE
New York

*First edition*

*Affiliate of*
MEREDITH PRESS
*Des Moines & New York*

Library of Congress Catalogue Card Number: 63-10357

MANUFACTURED IN THE UNITED STATES OF AMERICA FOR MEREDITH PRESS

VAN REES PRESS  •  NEW YORK

To

a father

and

his teenager

# Acknowledgments

If a writer were to award his own Medals of Honor, the recipients would be those who aided him "above and beyond the call of duty."

Special thanks are due to Captain Victor Gondos, Jr., Archivist in Charge, Civil War Records Branch, National Archives and Records Service, and Mr. Milton Chamberlain, Mrs. Sarah Jackson, and Mr. James Walker of his staff for making available the numerous official records of these teenage soldiers.

I am also indebted to Mr. Leon Weidman, Mrs. Shirley Spranger, and Mr. Frederick P. Willerford of the American History Collection, New York Public Library. The pages who served me so well there also deserve special recognition.

# Contents

☆  ☆  ☆

# THE BRAVEST TEENAGE YANKS

# CHAPTER I

## Teenagers in the Union Army

THE term "soldier boy," long in common usage, is meant to apply to any soldier, regardless of age. A "soldier boy" may therefore be between the ages of eighteen and forty-five, the minimum and maximum limits for enlistment in the United States Army. Men of those ages, however, can hardly be appropriately called "boys."

But during the Civil War the thousands of teenage soldiers in the Union Army were in every sense of the word boys. Asking and receiving no favors, they faithfully performed their military assignments in the ranks alongside their adult brothers-in-arms.

They underwent the rigors of army life in camp, on the march, and under the fire of the enemy, ignoring the fact that their very lives were often in danger. They mastered the use of rifle, musket, cannon, fife, bugle, and drum. Like their elders they were wounded in combat or succumbed to disease. They died on the battlefields or in hospitals.

To this day no one has been able to discover accurately how many teenagers wore the army blue. Eighteen was the legal minimum age for enlistment. Any boy under that age wanting to join up was required to present a release form containing the signed permission of his parent or guardian.

Thousands of underage youths are listed in the muster

rolls as below eighteen, evidently their true ages. However, the number of eighteen-year-olds is by far the highest of all ages in typical company and regimental rosters.

For this reason it is obvious that thousands of fifteen-, sixteen-, and seventeen-year-olds misrepresented their ages in order to be accepted by a recruiting officer, who was often only too glad to meet his quotas and fill up the ranks by asking no questions or requiring no proof of age.

Various studies on the ages of Union Army soldiers agree not on actual numbers but on percentages in each age group. Boys under eighteen appear to have made up about 1.3 per cent of all soldiers, or about 35,000.

From 10 to 13 per cent of the total of 2,750,000 enlistees, or about 300,000, were listed as exactly eighteen. Many of these were obviously considerably younger. The average age of all Union Army soldiers was a little over twenty-seven.

The typical Civil War soldier was therefore a young man.

To understand why so many teenagers went to war a hundred years ago it is necessary to understand the unique temper of the times. The secession of the eleven Southern states, from South Carolina in December, 1860, to Tennessee in June, 1861, meant that the United States was divided. Regardless of the reasons for these actions, most citizens of the Northern states took up the cry that the Union must be preserved. The teenagers naturally agreed with their elders.

After the fall of Fort Sumter in April, 1861, and the coming of war, the Northern objective became a glorious crusade to "save the Union." The quotas assigned to the states by the federal government in the first calls for volunteers were readily met.

Patriotism was at fever heat. Many a teenager shared the fire of patriotism that consumed his father, brother, relatives, neighbors, and friends, and which would not be quenched. Going to war was the thing to do, and the boys were determined to share in this absorbing adventure.

The formation of local companies served to strengthen the determination of the youths to join the army. The sounds of the drum, military commands, and the cadence of marching feet made many a young teenager's pulse beat faster. The call to the colors became irresistible.

When their parents would not sign the required release form after long hours of nagging, begging, and threatening, hundreds of lads ran away and lied about their ages. To avoid this threat, many a father took his underage boy with him in the army. Older brothers, relatives, or friends often acted as guardians for a young volunteer.

Most of the younger teenagers were enrolled as musicians—drummers and fifers—with the rank of private. Two such posts, which paid twelve dollars a month, were included in the organization of each company. These company musicians made up the fife and drum corps of the regiment.

The drummer boys and fifers were unarmed noncombatants. They took the place of men behind the lines during and after battles, aiding the wounded, acting as stretcher-bearers and hospital attendants and as couriers. Some became part-time orderlies to the top-grade officers.

In camp and on the long marches the taps and rolls of the drums were the "tongue of the army" (see Chapter 2). The life of the average drummer was in every way as rugged as that of the soldier except when it came to actual fighting.

The musicians in the cavalry and artillery were buglers. They were seldom below eighteen because they were mounted on horseback. This necessitated more stamina and experience than that required of the foot soldier of the infantry. A young boy often lacked the lung power to produce the bugle calls in camp and on the move above the clatter of the hoofbeats of the horses, and over the noises of battle.

A very large number of the Union Army teenagers, however, were privates carrying guns and using them in skirmishes, engagements, and full-scale battles. These boys were usually big for their ages. Many were rugged farm lads who possessed the necessary stamina for the life of the soldier. They had often been hunters, expert in the use of rifles and guns.

In a citizen army such as that of the United States in the Civil War, there were all types of soldiers. Fortunately, bearing arms came naturally to a large number; they adapted themselves to military life and formed the backbone of the volunteer army. Others, though well intentioned, failed to become good soldiers. As always, in any army, there were the cowards, the deserters, the laggards (called "skulkers" a century ago), and those who had gone to war to avoid the problems of civilian life.

The test of a good soldier begins with his arduous training, and continues through the monotony of army routines, the exhausting marches, and often insufficient and unattractive rations. But the final test comes under fire, when a soldier's mettle is put to the ultimate test.

To face the direct shot and shell of the enemy, to advance with pointed bayonet in the face of murderous fire, to see one's fellows fall wounded or dead, demands more than mere devotion to duty. It requires fearlessness, bravery, and courage. The most intrepid fighters admit to occasional fear, particularly when under fire for the first time.

The truly courageous soldier casts aside all feelings of fear when an objective is to be achieved. He summons all his powers of concentration to the immediate situation. Sometimes this is automatic; more often it represents a definite, almost superhuman effort on his part.

When a soldier exhibits uncommon courage or bravery in performing deeds of daring in the presence of danger and at the risk of his life, as in battle, his act becomes one of heroism. He has exhibited a fearlessness and daring transcending common sense, self-preservation, and judgment.

Thousands of Civil War soldiers, both Confederate and Union, performed such exceptional deeds of heroism and valor. Many were cited in official dispatches and reports. Some were given field promotions on the spot. A selected few obtained special recognition by receiving the nation's highest military honor, the Army Medal of Honor.

European countries had long decorated their military heroes. But the United States lagged far behind except for a few special medals awarded during the Revolution. In December, 1861, when the Civil War had barely begun, a Navy Medal was authorized for enlisted sailors.

In 1862 the United States Congress authorized a Medal of Honor to be awarded to enlisted men of the regular army and the volunteer forces who "shall most distinguish themselves by their gallantry in action, and other soldier-like qualities." Approved by President Lincoln on July 12, 1862, the act became law and was extended the next year to include officers as well as enlisted men.

The Medal of Honor, often erroneously called the Congressional Medal of Honor, was awarded to about twelve hundred Civil War soldiers in the Union Army. Many were not conferred until many years after the war, as late as the 1890's, when the veterans were middle-aged or old men. To date, a total of over twenty-three hundred awards have been made (Civil War, Indian and frontier campaigns, the Spanish-American War, World War I and II, and the Korean War).

After the Civil War, the qualifications were made more specific: "for a deed of personal bravery or self sacrifice above and beyond the call of duty while a member of the armed forces in actual combat with an enemy of the nation."

A recommendation for a medal was to be accompanied by the testimony of three eye-witnesses of the act. It is from these descriptions, now in the files of the National Archives in Washington, that one may obtain the details. Other records, personal narratives, and military and local histories fill in the information on the individual medal winners.

The medal was engraved on its reverse side with the name and rank of the soldier, his organization, and the place and date of the act for which it was awarded. At first it was to be worn around the neck on a blue silk ribbon. Later a rosette was supplied for the buttonhole, then a ribbon to be worn on the left breast. A written citation, describing the act (such as those in the following chapter headings of this book), was given to the winner.

Though legislation was enacted in 1862 by the Confederate Congress for a war medal to be issued to the bravest of the Southern soldiers, none were ever conferred. Because of the difficulties in procuring medals and badges, a Roll of Honor was substituted, published in General Orders, listing the names of those soldiers who "have best displayed their courage and devotion on the field of battle."

These Rolls were published only three times, and discontinued after December, 1864. About two thousand soldiers were cited, many of whom were killed before the war was ended. This honor, however, was always known as the Confederate Medal of Honor, and is so named whenever it is mentioned on muster rolls and other official records.

Thousands of courageous soldiers in our wars did not receive the Medal of Honor, still the highest military award for bravery that can be given to any individual in the United States of America. The number of medals bestowed would be multiplied many times had every act performed "above and beyond the call of duty" been recognized.

The teenage Civil War winners in the chapters following are not the only soldiers of that age group to receive Medals of Honor, though all known to be under sixteen years old at the time of their act of bravery are included. A few sixteen- and seventeen-year-olds have been selected because their exploits were particularly impressive. At least six other six-teen-year-olds, eleven who were seventeen, and ten aged eighteen received the medal for Civil War acts.

These "bravest teenage Yanks" were ordinary soldiers, many with several years' experience in the Union Army. They came from country and city. Their army service proved that they were boys doing men's work, and that their "sol-dier-like qualities" were of the highest order.

# CHAPTER 2

## *The Youngest Medal Winner*

JOHNSTON, WILLIE. Musician, Company D, 3rd Vermont Infantry.

For bravery in Eastern Virginia, May-June 1862 (when he was twelve years old).

Citation: "Gallantry in the Seven Days' Fight and Peninsular Campaign."

Born Morristown, St. Lawrence County, N.Y., 1850.

Mustered in, 1 May 1862; mustered out, 31 August 1865.

Award made on 16 September 1863.

WITH a very few exceptions Medals of Honor were awarded to Union Army soldiers for specific acts of bravery. Citations for only a scant dozen of the Civil War winners were for conduct during a campaign or a battle, reading "Gallantry in action," "Distinguished bravery in action," or "Unparalleled bravery under fire."

One of these nonspecific awards was made to the youngest soldier ever to win the medal in its century-old history, Willie Johnston, a drummer boy in a Vermont regiment. His citation was based on the fact that during one of the crucial campaigns of the Union Army of the Potomac, in which scores of drummer boys participated, he was the only one to retain his drum to the very end of the series of battles.

This award made to twelve-year-old William Johnston (officially listed as Willie Johnston) was actually a recognition of the faithful services of the thousands of drummers in the Union Army and their indispensability.

The term "drummer boy" brings to mind a handsome, smiling, fuzzy-cheeked youngster in resplendent spick-and-span uniform, carrying a large parade or snare drum decorated with a painted American or regimental flag with the number of the unit on it. Such a picture was true only in parades and reviews, for during most of their army service the duties of the musicians were fully as arduous as those of the soldiers, and the length of their ordinary day even longer.

When he first joined a company the drummer was put to work immediately. He played when the recruits drilled and fixed the time for the step when the regiment marched off to war.

In camp he regulated the routines. His instrument was called "the tongue of the camp," for his calls and rolls took the place of verbal commands in those days long before the introduction of loud-speakers, walkie-talkies, and sound systems in modern armies. The bugle performed the same functions in the cavalry and artillery.

The drummer's day began before daybreak, at four or five o'clock, when the "drummer's call" was beaten near the guard tents by the Principal Musician. That was the signal for all drummers to assemble before the colors of the regiment in front of the headquarters, where they beat out the "reveille." This summoned all the soldiers to form in line to report for morning roll call. A little later they beat the "breakfast call."

At eight o'clock came the "sergeant's" or "sick call," summoning those soldiers who sought to be excused from duty because of illness or who had other nonmilitary business.

This was often termed the "quinine" call, because, like aspirin today, quinine was given by the army doctors in the Civil War for almost every ordinary ailment.

At nine o'clock the drummers beat the "guard mount" and followed by marking time for the soldiers at squad, company, or battalion drill, tapping out the rhythms for the double-quick, wheeling (turns), and the like. They then sounded the "dinner call," the main meal of the day in camp being at noon. The afternoon was comparatively free except for practice and additional duties as orderlies to the officers of highest rank.

Summoning the men with another "dinner call" at five o'clock, they laid aside their drumsticks for the knife and fork, after which they beat the "evening roll call" at eight o'clock, calling the soldiers to the color-line for dress parade.

After this ceremony the soldiers were dismissed for the night, and the drummers waited another hour before sounding "tattoo," the signal to prepare for sleep. The day ended with "taps" ("lights out") gently beat by each company drummer going down the line of tents. The bugle "taps" composed by General Daniel Butterfield in July, 1862, replaced the many separate and noisy drum beats, and was intended to bring comfort and peace to the tired soldiers at the end of the day.

This daily camp routine was an experience shared by all drummers, for a large part of the soldiers' service was spent in camp between campaigns and engagements. The longest such period was the winter, when few battles were fought.

Until bands were abolished in mid-1862, the company drummers were also band members. Thereafter, unless a musical organization could be assembled from the ranks, drummers and fifers supplied the music for parades and reviews. All the musicians of a regiment were trained and controlled by a Principal Musician who was on the regimental staff.

The drummers beat the "long roll" as a signal to break camp, to prepare to move, or to meet the enemy. This might be at any time—in the middle of the night, before dawn, or during the day. But when battles were imminent, the drums were silenced so that the enemy would not discover the nearness of unfriendly troops.

On long marches the drummers served as morale builders. When the soldiers were trudging along the road with weary limbs and bodies, the drummer boys, though equally tired, would keep the soldiers in step with their drum beats—left, right, left, right, left, right—lifting the men's low spirits and stirring them to carry on.

Since many Civil War drummers were young teenagers, mastery of the drum might seem to be easy. But such was not the case. The technique involved many types of beats and different tempos. The art of drumming had a glossary of terms all its own—rolls, strokes, flams, drags, ruffle or ruffles, paradiddles, and the ratamacue. The drummers were therefore required to practice almost daily under the tutelage of the Principal Musician. Almost all became expert.

During battles the drummer boys, with white patches on their sleeves to identify them as noncombatants, looked after the wounded and helped in carrying them on litters or stretchers to ambulances and field hospitals, where some of the lads even assisted the surgeons in operations and amputations. These duties compelled them to be under fire frequently, and many a youth impetuously seized a gun and went into action with the older soldiers.

Drummers were generally teenagers, for every adult soldier was needed as a fighting man. The term "drummer boy" was therefore more exact than "soldier boy."

Willie Johnston was not the very youngest drummer boy in the Union Army. Records reveal several younger—a few, amazingly enough, only eight years old. But not many were younger than Willie, and his record proved that he was the equal of many drummers who were older.

In the late 1840's, William Johnston, the boy's father, who bore the same name (hence the use of "Willie" for his son), emigrated to this country from Nottingham, England, as a newlywed. The couple settled on a farm in northern New York State. In 1850 Willie was born in Morristown, a village on the St. Lawrence River.

His mother died when Willie was still an infant. He was only three years old when his father remarried. His stepmother was a French-Canadian girl from Montreal.

Very soon the family moved eastward to Salem, Vermont, just south of the Canadian border and near the New Hampshire state line. After the war the village was incorporated into the township of Derby, and so is no longer found on maps. Life was hard and lonely on the farm, for it was difficult to make a living from the rocky land.

When all of Vermont was alive with patriotism after the fall of Fort Sumter, the towns vied with one another in furnishing more men than the quotas assigned them by the Governor. One of the inducements was the payment of local bounties, a certain sum of money offered for enlisting.

A village like Salem could not compete with a large town like St. Johnsbury in the next county, which offered $187.50 bounty money (the equivalent of $500 today). A history of Salem expressed it this way: *A large number of the citizens of Salem enlisted to the credit of other towns in which money was more abundant than patriotism.*

So it was that Mr. Johnston, then forty years of age, enlisted on June 1 as a private in Company B of the 3rd Vermont Infantry, credited to St. Johnsbury. He received an additional government bounty of $100. Mustered in in mid-July, he was off to the wars.

Like many another youngster whose father was at the front, Willie rebelled at remaining on the farm with his stepmother. Father and son became increasingly lonesome for one another as the months of separation passed.

While acting as the regimental color-bearer at Lees Mills, Virginia, on the sixteenth of April, 1862, Private Johnston was wounded. This was the charge upon the enemy's fortifications and rifle pits across Warwick Creek, the same in which Julian Scott of the same regiment (Chapter 10) won his Medal of Honor.

While recuperating in a field hospital, Johnston more than ever wanted to see his son. The easiest way was for Willie to enlist as a fellow-soldier in the 3rd Vermont.

Medical discharges, wounds, and death had caused the regiment to become under-strength, and several drummer-boy posts were vacant. So Mr. Johnston sent home a signed release form for Willie, telling him to go to St. Johnsbury and enlist. This the boy did on the first day of May, becoming a musician in Company D. Young as he was, he received both the town and government bounty, which he sent home to his stepmother. His age was entered on the rolls as fourteen, though he was actually two years younger.

A brave and resolute little fellow, Willie caught up with his father's regiment in Virginia and found himself immediately involved in the continuous battles of the Peninsular Campaign of the Union Army of the Potomac, commanded by General George McClellan. The objective of this thrust was to advance on Richmond, the Confederate capital, up the James River Peninsula from Fort Monroe.

During the last of May and early June, Willie took part in the fiercely fought battles of Fair Oaks and Seven Pines to the west of Richmond.

Throughout the last week of June, the two great armies were locked in desperate conflict in the Seven Days' Battles before Richmond. These almost continuous contests were characterized by tremendous numbers of opposing troops fighting major battles almost daily, with huge casualty tolls of dead and wounded.

The Southerners were determined to defend their capital to the death, and the Northerners were equally determined to capture it as a first step in hastening the end of the war and the downfall of the Confederacy.

McClellan's army, numbering ninety-two thousand men, was within a few miles of the city, which was defended by General Lee with an army of eighty thousand.

A major battle was fought daily, resulting in draws or narrow victories. Their names—Mechanicsville, Gaines' Mill, Savage's Station, White Oak Swamp, and Malvern Hill—call up memories of the bloodiest and most closely fought battles of the entire war. A foreign observer said of these Seven Days' Battles, "It was no war—it was murder."

In this single week before July 1, the Army of the Potomac lost 1,700 killed, 8,000 wounded, and 6,000 captured and missing. The Confederate loss was 3,500 killed, 16,000 wounded, and 875 captured and missing.

All through the bloody, violent days, the 3rd Vermont Regiment marched all night and fought all day. One of the sergeants wrote home that for five successive days and nights he was able to snatch not more than ten hours of sleep.

Such was Willie Johnston's experience during those June days in Virginia, and only his stamina and grit carried him through the ordeal which felled many a soldier twice or thrice his age.

The campaign ended in a draw. After more than a month of continuous fighting, the Union forces made a strategical retreat to Harrison's Landing, on the James River south of Richmond. Those who did not want to admit how close the Army of the Potomac had come to defeat and rout termed this mass movement a "change of base." The plan was to rest and rebuild the shattered regiments before attacking Petersburg, to the south of Richmond.

Within two months as a tenderfoot soldier, Willie Johnston had been under fire more often than many a seasoned
veteran, and more than most drummers during their entire
army service. The battles had been fought in forests and
swamplands, with frontal assaults and flank attacks. Artillery bombardment was more than normally fierce. The hardships were increased by heavy rainfall and overhanging fog,
and the troops wallowed in seas of mud.

On the way to Harrison's Landing the soldiers staggered
through field, swamps, brush, and heavy woods, for the roads
were impassable. Pioneer troops were cutting trees to be
used in "corduroying" the muddy roads.

The drummers had constantly beat out the "long roll"
as a call to action. In the retreat to the new base many a
soldier discarded his gun, haversack, and blankets, even ammunition, so that he might have less weight to carry. The
eighty exhausted drummers of the regiments in Willie's division threw away their drums along the way. When the
division set up camp, Willie Johnston was the only one who
had brought his drum with him from the field.

From all the areas where the recent battles had been
fought the battered remnants of the once proud Army of
the Potomac reassembled at Harrison's Landing, literally
staggering for the last few miles. Most of them poured into
camp on July 2.

What awaited them was a worthy reward for weary,
battle-torn soldiers. A huge area along the James River had
been cleared and laid out in regular order. Each division
was assigned its own space, in which all its regiments were
encamped together.

Shelter and wall tents had been pitched in even lines along
company streets. Most of them had plank floors. But what
made the camp seem like heaven to the utterly exhausted
Yanks were the individual beds and cots, an almost forgotten

luxury which many of them had not enjoyed for several months.

The clean, pure water, so different from the brackish swamp water they had been drinking, was ambrosia. Many of the soldiers had not had a complete bath for at least a month. Almost all had not taken off their uniforms for five weeks. Their bodies were caked with dirt and mud, their feet swollen and blistered, their filthy clothing crawling with lice.

After roll call, the officers wisely dismissed the men for twenty-four hours. Long lines formed near the improvised showers and water barrels, and the banks of the James River were crowded with bathers. Fresh rations were enjoyed as if they were the finest delicacies. Then the soldiers fell into the clean beds. In the silence of the vast camp, such a contrast with the accustomed battle noise, many slept around the clock.

The third of July was like a holiday. The very recent order abolishing bands had not yet been acted upon. The discarded drums were not immediately replaced. So the men were awakened by band music, the first played for them since the last of May. This soon put the physically refreshed troops in good humor. By afternoon the drums and bugles of the band members began to sound the familiar calls, according to one soldier, "making us happy again."

An announcement from General McClellan was circulated on this day to all the corps and divisions:

> A national salute will be fired at noon tomorrow, at the headquarters of each army corps. Immediately thereafter the bands will play appropriate national airs. The general commanding will visit all the troops during the afternoon when the troops will be paraded and a Major General's salute fired in each corps.

As a reward for being the only one to bring his drum safely through the arduous campaign, Willie Johnston was chosen to be the sole drummer in the review for General McClellan on that holiday afternoon. Proudly he beat out the rhythm of the steps when the several thousand surviving soldiers of the division paraded for their Commanding General and their corps, division, and regimental leaders.

One of the soldiers reported:

> The review in the afternoon was quite a success. The men looked well, their clothes a little shabby, but altogether soldierly and businesslike ... Instead of the usual competing noise of the various drum corps, our little Willie made the music for our marching. The band played later as the troops were drawn up and Little Mac passed between the lines.

The divisional commander, General William "Baldy" Smith, was from St. Albans, Vermont, and he was so pleased with his twelve-year-old fellow citizen's fidelity and pluck that he mentioned Willie's name in dispatches to the War Department.

Legislation for the Medal of Honor had not yet been enacted. But over a year later, in September, 1863, Willie was summoned to Washington by Adjutant General Townsend, who took him to the War Department and introduced him to Secretary of War Stanton.

On the spot Stanton wrote a short note: *Willie Johnston, Musician, Company D, 3rd Vermont Volunteers, is to receive the Medal of Honor for gallantry in the Seven Days' Fight and the Peninsular Campaign.* Townsend returned to his office and passed on the instructions to his Chief Clerk for action. The engraving was completed within two days. When Willie returned to his regiment at the end of his furlough he proudly wore the medal on its ribbon around his neck.

Because of his youth and this recognition as one of the first of the medal winners, Willie Johnston became a celebrity. The soldiers were curious to see the little drummer boy. Therefore for the next few months, on detached duty, he went to the divisions and corps throughout the Army of the Potomac, exhibiting his skill with the drumsticks in dress parades and demonstrating the various calls before the high brass and their wives in many a camp.

Though he was usually completely at ease in such company, Willie squirmed with embarrassment when the women sought to cuddle and kiss him while making personal remarks on his manly bearing and diminutive size.

On the fifteenth of February, 1864, the father and son re-enlisted at Brandy Station, Virginia, and spent a thirty-day furlough at home in Vermont. Willie was transferred to Company H, but was soon separated from his father. Private Johnston, having lost his right-hand trigger finger from a gunshot wound, could no longer shoot a gun, and was therefore transferred to engineering work.

On the way back to his regiment from his leave, Willie stopped off to see some of the high-ranking sponsors in Washington, and obtained a transfer to the 20th Regiment of the Veteran Reserve Corps as drum major, a high honor for a fourteen-year-old.

But very soon he was ordered back to his original regiment and company, the reason being given that he was too young to be a veteran! He was, however, a veteran volunteer (the term for a soldier who re-enlisted) and was so listed in Company H.

His father was mustered out of the army during the last of July, 1865, after four years of service. Willie left the army the next month. He had been a soldier for three years and four months, and yet was only a little over fifteen years old!

Very little is known of the postwar life of the Johnstons. The father died in 1902, after wandering through the western states for many years. Young Willie returned to Salem and was farming twenty-five acres in 1880. No further local record is available. Since he never applied for the government benefits for which he was eligible—a pension and the special monthly payment as a Medal of Honor winner—it can be assumed that he died when still comparatively young.

At any rate, Willie Johnston had his day of glory at a time when most boys are still in the schoolroom, and his name lives as the youngest of the Medal of Honor winners both during the Civil War and throughout its hundred-year history.

# CHAPTER 3

## *The Lifesaver*

HORSFALL, WILLIAM H. Drummer, Company G, 1st Kentucky Infantry.

For act of bravery at Corinth, Mississippi, 21 May 1862 (when he was fourteen years and three months old).

Citation: "Saved the life of a wounded officer lying between the lines."

Born Newport, Kentucky, 3 March 1848.

Mustered in, 31 December 1861; mustered out, 19 August 1864.

Award made on 17 August 1895.

ONE of the tragedies to the individual of a civil war is the difficulty of choosing where his loyalty lies. During the internal struggle of the early 1860's, the choice was easy and natural for those who lived far within the boundaries of either the loyal states or the Confederacy.

New Englanders, for example, never faced the decision, for they had few ties with the Southland. On the other hand, residents of the deep South, with some few exceptions—and those mainly based on their attitudes toward the institution of slavery—allied themselves unquestionably with their neighbors who were Confederates.

In the border states, however, the decision of which side to support was more complicated. Delaware, Maryland, Missouri, and Kentucky were to remain divided throughout the entire war, offering troops to both the North and the South. The western portion of Virginia parted from the mother state early in the war, forming the new state of West Virginia when the war had reached midpoint. Missouri was the setting of a bitter internal strife, almost a war within a war.

The Ohio River formed Kentucky's northern border, 650 miles long. Directly opposite its broad waters from west to east were the loyal states of Illinois, Indiana, and Ohio to the north and what was to become Union Virginia (West Virginia) on the east. The southern boundary adjoined Tennessee, the southeast, Confederate Virginia.

Because of its geographical location, Kentucky became a keystone between the two sections, but in reality belonged to neither, some said to both. Its neutrality was declared a month after the beginning of the conflict with the official statement that "the state will take no part in the Civil War now being waged." The internal division of the allegiance of its citizens, however, continued throughout the struggle, and in no other state were there so many examples of divided families.

The split was more serious because the two Presidents—Abraham Lincoln and Jefferson Davis—were born in Kentucky within a year of and only one hundred miles from each other. The state's neutrality, however, existed only on paper, and the internal struggle continued throughout the long war.

The northern part was strongly pro-Union because of both the proximity to and economic ties with the North. Campbell County, to the south of Cincinnati, was in the northernmost section of the state.

The town of Newport, in Campbell County, was directly opposite Cincinnati, which was a center for the enlistment of soldiers from southern Ohio. The sympathies of the family of William H. Horsfall, who was born on the third of March, 1848, in Newport, Kentucky, lay with the Union cause. Early in the war many a Kentuckian crossed the river and enlisted as a soldier in an Ohio regiment. They were at that time counted in the Ohio quotas. As the state's neutrality was violated by both the North and South, local feeling reached a high pitch of excitement.

Kentucky Unionists of military age formed several companies, which were refused by the state during its period of neutrality. These loyal men crossed the river to Camp Clay, near Cincinnati, where Union troops were organized for training and mustering.

President Lincoln consented to receive these Kentuckians into the Union Army as the 1st and 2nd Kentucky Volunteer Infantry, equipped and prepared at the expense of Ohio, and later recognized by their native state.

Observing the continuous embarkation of these soldiers at the Newport wharves throughout the late fall of 1861, young Billy Horsfall became determined to be a soldier boy. When his parents turned a deaf ear to his appeals, he ran away without any warning to them, and without money.

On the twentieth of December, in company with three of his schoolmates, the lad stealthily boarded the steamer *Annie Laurie,* moored at a Newport wharf. After a stop at Cincinnati, the boat was to go on eastward to the Kanawha River in the loyal section of Virginia.

Billy Horsfall was not sure of his destination. He knew only that somehow he *must* wear the Union blue.

While the steamer was loading, Billy's three chums had a change of heart. To their way of thinking the future was too indefinite. Their courage and determination suddenly waned.

"We're not going, Billy," they finally said in unison. "What will our families do when they discover we are gone?

How do we know whether we will be accepted in the army? Suppose we are sent back home—what then?"

"*You* can do what you like," retorted Billy, "but *I* am leaving." They wavered momentarily until the bell rang signaling the departure of the boat, and a sailor called out "All ashore who are going ashore!" The three lads rans down the gangplank just as it was about to be hauled aboard, and waved to their more daring friend until the *Annie Laurie* nosed from the dock and headed across the river.

Billy Horsfall kept in hiding until the boat was well under way and then ventured on deck. *I was accosted by the captain of the boat as to my destination,* he later wrote, *and telling him the old orphan-boy story, I was treated very kindly, given something to eat, and allowed very liberal privileges.*

Disembarking at Cincinnati, he had no difficulty in being directed to Camp Clay, where he expected to find the two Kentucky infantry regiments. But, to his dismay, they had long since moved on to western Virginia, and by then had even taken part in some of the battles fought in what was then the District of Kanawha.

This disappointment posed a problem for Billy. He could very easily return home, to be welcomed by his family with joyous relief. Or he could catch up with the regiments.

Though still penniless and with only the clothes he was wearing, Billy hesitated but a short time before making his decision. He would go on with his plan to join the Kentuckians in the Union Army.

Admiring the resoluteness of the youngster, friendly Ohio recruits at the camp gave him rations and pocket money and helped him on his way. He accompanied some newly mustered companies by troop transport up the Ohio River, then down the Kanawha to the District Army Headquarters.

By a stroke of good luck the young drummer of Company G, 1st Kentucky Volunteer Infantry, had recently been discharged because of illness. The commander was so delighted to have an eager replacement that he asked no questions and suspended all the usual requirements, enrolling Billy on the last day of the year.

Private Horsfall was then thirteen years and ten months old, recorded on the rolls as fourteen. He was exceptionally small—only four feet three inches in height—a towhead with blue eyes. He agreed to serve out the remainder of the regiment's three-year enlistment term.

Because of his diminutive size, Billy had some difficulty in being fitted with a uniform. He rolled up the cuffs of his trousers several times. His oversize jacket clung in many folds over his tightened belt. There were no government issue shoes small enough for his feet, and though he stuffed the oversize shoes with cotton, his feet were soon a mass of infected blisters. As a result he seldom wore shoes during his military service, preferring to be barefoot.

His drum was so large that he constantly stumbled over it on marches. Even when the leather straps were shortened the drum banged against his knees so constantly that they developed huge calluses. These physical difficulties, however, had little effect on his soldierly bearing and enthusiasm. He had yearned for the life of a soldier boy and was ready to accept its hardships without complaint.

During the early months of 1862 the regiment was on guard duty at Nashville but was soon rushed east to join forces with scores of other units under General Grant. A Confederate thrust to regain their losses in Tennessee led to one of the bloodiest battles of the war at Shiloh (Pittsburg Landing), Tennessee, on the sixth and seventh of April.

Here Billy underwent his baptism of fire, putting away his drum for a gun in disregard of the usual rule that musicians should remain to the rear beyond the range of gunfire. His company was officially cited for its part in the battle: *Com-*

*pany G was in full range of the enemy's fire and at all times maintained its formation with a tenacity becoming veterans.*

On the second day at Shiloh the Confederate forces, after ten hours of bitter fighting, were driven south across the state boundary line to Corinth, Mississippi, where they prepared to make a stand. The 1st Kentucky Regiment followed with the Union Army of the Tennessee, and a siege began at the end of the month.

The Northern strength in front of Corinth was over a hundred thousand men against sixty-five thousand Southerners determined not to be pushed farther south. It was in one of the skirmishes of this campaign that Billy Horsfall performed the act "above and beyond the call of duty" which won him the Medal of Honor many years later.

The 1st Kentucky was near the house of a widow named Serratt, a little over a mile from Corinth and a few miles from the Tennessee border to the north. By then Billy had become an expert sharpshooter, acting independently of his company when the regiment was in combat. His company commander apparently approved of his preference for the gun to the drum when under fire. Billy was understandably proud of his heavy twenty-pound sniper rifle with telescopic sight, with which he could "draw a bead" on an enemy soldier with devastating results.

On the late afternoon of May 20, two of the regiment's companies were sent into the woods to the left of the other units, with orders to prevent the enemy from approaching from the rear, while the remaining companies advanced behind skirmishers.

Before the soldiers of Company H had proceeded more than a hundred yards in a charge across a ravine, they encountered extremely heavy and concentrated enemy fire.

Three times the Confederates tried to drive them from their position, but the Kentuckians heroically held their ground. Seventeen men fell wounded, several severely.

The Captain, James Williamson, fell from a severe bullet wound in the hip. Even while lying on the ground, he continued to direct the movements of his men. But immediately the Confederates gained the advantage, forcing the attackers to retreat, leaving the officer on the field between the cross fire. Unable to move enough to crawl to safety, he was in serious danger of being captured.

Williamson's subordinate, Lieutenant Louis Hocke, approached Billy and shouted above the din, "Horsfall, Captain Williamson is in trouble! Rescue him if possible!"

Leaning his rifle against a tree, the drummer boy turned soldier, in a stooping run, reached the Captain's side while bullets peppered the ground all around him.

"Captain," he shouted, "relax and I'll do the rest. Don't worry! I'll get you to safety!"

Seizing the half-conscious officer by the wrists, the boy began dragging the Captain across the field, over others who had fallen. Because of the low-hanging smoke, Billy could not tell whether he was passing enemy or friendly soldiers. The noise of the discharging muskets was deafening, and he could recognize neither friend nor foe. A stream of blood from the Captain's open wound marked his slow progress.

Captain Williamson was a heavy man, and his rescuer was forced to stop to rest from time to time. But in moments of crisis a sudden and almost superhuman strength can often be summoned. Little Billy was no exception. Slowly and steadily he crossed the field, passing through the fighting Kentucky soldiers who were attempting to halt the enemy's advance.

Before he was even aware of the distance he had covered, Billy with his human burden reached the waiting stretcher-bearers, and Captain Williamson was immediately carried to the rear, where a surgeon tended his fresh wound.

After the battle, Private Horsfall dismissed his comrades' words of praise for his act. "I was only obeying the Lieutenant's order," was all he would say.

During all the later marches and engagements of the 1st Kentucky Billy continued to prove himself a dependable soldier. Most of his fellow-soldiers forgot his youth and small size. His actions had made a man of him in their eyes.

The regiment's next major battle was at Stone River, near Murfreesboro, Tennessee, on the last day of the year, the first anniversary of Billy's enlistment. The 1st Kentucky was ordered to move forward when an Indiana regiment in an open field in front of them ran out of ammunition. They were caught in the enemy's artillery fire and came under vigorous attack from the Confederates directly in front of them.

In the confusion young Horsfall was separated from his company, lost his canteen and haversack, and found himself hemmed in by both enemy cavalry and infantry. Determined not to surrender, he decided to run for his life. Even the Southerners took pity on his youth and were reluctant to shoot at the little chap though he was a direct and easy target.

While Billy was scampering to safety like a lively little monkey, one of the Johnnies called out to his fellows, "Don't shoot the little Yank. I want him for a cage!" Plucky little Billy reached his regiment in safety. The top Union commander, General William "Rosey" Rosecrans, personally complimented him for his bravery.

Later, in September, 1863, the 1st Kentucky fought furiously against almost unsurmountable odds at Chickamauga, Georgia, where Billy's company again received an official citation. The Kentuckians next participated in the first stage of the Atlanta campaign and later returned to duty in their home state, being discharged when their three-year enlistment term expired in July, 1864.

After the Battle of Stone River the hardships and rigors

of army life began exacting their toll on Billy Horsfall, and he spent the first two months of 1863 in a Nashville military hospital.

On his application for a furlough when he recovered, the General of his division wrote: *Approved. A nice little lad who wants to stay in the service. He is a good drummer and a brave boy. At Stone River he got a gun and some cartridges and went into the fight. I encountered him firing and had him sent to the rear.*

His Colonel forwarded the request to higher headquarters with the notation: *The boy is a little man, a fine drummer and anxious to serve his term of enlistment.* After twenty days at home in Newport, where he found that his family had forgiven him for running away, he returned to his regiment.

When the 1st Kentucky was to be mustered out in Covington after completing its service, there was some question as to whether Billy was eligible for discharge. Since he had joined the regiment when it had already seen several months of service, it was necessary to explain that he had enlisted with the understanding that he would serve only the uncompleted term of the 1st Kentucky. A special dispensation was therefore requested in his case.

*He is but fifteen years old,* his Captain wrote to the War Department, *and has always been a manly, faithful soldier. Having served over two and a half years he is desirous of going to school.* And so he was given his discharge on the nineteenth of August, 1864, a veteran soldier when sixteen and a half.

As was true of many another soldier boy, Billy's rigorous service while he was still in the early years of adolescence later affected his health. By middle age he was a semi-invalid, with rheumatism and a heart condition.

Congressman Albert S. Berry of Kentucky recommended Mr. Horsfall as worthy to receive the Medal of Honor for his brave act under fire on that May day thirty-three years before when he was but three months over fourteen. Representative Berry had served in the Confederate Army, but by that time the old enmities had been forgiven, if not forgotten.

Horsfall wrote to Mr. Berry:

What may have been our attitude in the past, I hope and sincerely believe we are now welded firmly and forever in the bonds of friendship and national unity under the flag. . . . I value my record [he continued] not as a victor over the vanquished but as a personal vindication of my fidelity to the cause under which I enrolled and would desire it just the same had I followed the leadership of the famous heroes Lee and Jackson.

When Billy Horsfall received his Medal of Honor in 1895, he expressed his thanks in a letter addressed to "His Excellency the President and the Congress, at Washington, D.C.":

Greetings of love and good will to all. Accept my expressions of gratitude and thanks for the handsome and valuable token of your appreciation of my services. I shall always wear it with a remembrance that it came from the best republic in the world and for services in defense of a flag that contains more patriotic inspiration than any other beneath the sun.

For many years thereafter Mr. Horsfall proudly wore his Medal around his neck on its blue ribbon when the local Grand Army of the Republic veterans marched in Newport's Memorial Day and Fourth of July parades. He married in 1871, and his children numbered six.

Death came to Mr. Horsfall in 1922 when he was almost seventy-five years old, sixty years after the time when he performed the act fitting the requirements for the Medal of Honor—"a deed of personal bravery or self sacrifice above and beyond the call of duty."

# CHAPTER 4

# *The Ammunition-Bearer*

HOWE, ORION P. Musician, Company C, 55th Illinois Infantry.

For act of bravery at Vicksburg, Mississippi, 19 May 1863 (when he was fourteen years and five months old).

Citation: "A drummer boy, 14 years of age, and severely wounded and exposed to a heavy fire from the enemy, he persistently remained upon the field of battle until he had reported to General W. T. Sherman the necessity of supplying cartridges for the use of troops under the command of Colonel Malmborg."

Born Hiram, Ohio, 29 December 1848.

Mustered in, 21 September 1862; mustered out, 1 October 1864.

Award made on 23 April 1896.

WHEN his wife died at the family farm near Hiram, Portage County, Ohio, in 1852, farmer William H. Howe was left with two motherless sons, Lyston, aged two, and Orion, four. His sister and her husband offered to give the little boys a home and a woman's care, so the three Howes went to live at a farm near Waukegan, Illinois, a small town north of Chicago.

Waukegan and Lake County, in which it was located, responded to President Lincoln's first call for volunteers in April, 1861, by recruiting a company of soldiers, most of them farmers. Mr. Howe had served in the United States Army during the Mexican War, rising in the ranks from fifer to Major. It was natural for him to be one of the first to enlist. Since each volunteer company elected its own officers in those early days of the war, his previous rank meant nothing. He therefore signed up for three years as a private in Company I of the 15th Illinois Infantry Regiment.

Lyston was then within three months of being eleven years old, while Orion was twelve and a half. The boys had often listened, wide-eyed and open-mouthed, to their father's accounts of his experiences in Texas and Mexico in 1848, and begged that he take them with him.

But if all three went to war the farm work could not be done, for all the local young men were joining the army. So it was finally decided that Orion, being the eldest, husky and strong for his age and a good worker, would stay at home and help his uncle.

Lyston had learned to drum, and Mr. Howe proposed to the recruiting officer that he and his son serve as a team of fifer and drummer in Company I. On June fifth his father signed the required consent form and Lyston was officially entered on the muster roll honestly as ten years nine months and nine days, his height four feet two inches, both, of course, far below the minimum requirement.

Father and son went with the regiment to Missouri. In the late fall, like many another youngster in the army, Lyston contracted measles, then pneumonia. While the boy was in an army hospital at Tipton, his father went to St. Louis on a furlough.

There Fifer Howe met many friends from his home county in the 55th Illinois Infantry Regiment. To be with them he applied for and received a transfer to Company C and was assigned to the post of Principal Musician of the regiment, with supervision over the fifers and drummers in the various companies.

Lyston had meanwhile been discharged "for youthfulness," so his father wrote from Paducah, Kentucky, telling him to return home to Waukegan when he was well enough to make the trip. Orion looked forward to a reunion with his brother.

But going home was the last thing in the world the young soldier wanted to do. So, drum and all, Lyston evaded his nurses one night, ran away from the hospital, and joined his father after a month-long journey. Mr. Howe was really pleased that his son wanted to continue with him, though he rebuked Lyston sternly for his disobedience. He boasted openly and proudly of his son's accomplishment in making the long trip from Missouri alone.

There was a vacant post as drummer in Company B, so Lyston began filling it on February 12, 1862.

As each bit of news from his father and younger brother reached Orion in Waukegan, he became increasingly restless. His father's account of the regiment's first time under fire at the Battle of Shiloh in April, when the 55th Illinois tangled successfully with a Confederate force five times its number, made him envious. More than ever he yearned to smell the smoke of battle.

The routine farm chores seemed monotonous compared with what Orion heard about the excitement of army life. Furthermore, he was lonesome for his family. Try as they would, his aunt and uncle could not replace his absent father and brother, and they sensed his restlessness.

The determined lad finally decided that the only way he could hope to join the army was to learn to drum. From a Chicago music publishing firm Orion purchased a copy of the official instruction book for army drummers. He began practicing during the late spring. If he became expert, he reasoned, his father would permit him to join the 55th, then stationed at Memphis.

Orion and his drum became inseparable. Hearing the frequent clatter in the upstairs bedroom and even in the fields, his aunt and uncle realized that their nephew was resolutely determined to leave Waukegan. They even wrote Mr. Howe about his son's intention, pointing out Orion's half-hearted performance of the farm chores and suggesting that the necessary permission be granted.

But the father still felt that Orion's place was on the farm. Even though he worked listlessly, he was still a substitute for the two absent Howes.

As weeks lengthened into months, Orion, chafing under his colorless daily routines, could finally endure it no longer. So one evening in the late summer of 1862, without even leaving a note for his aunt and uncle, the would-be soldier lad ran away to join his father and brother.

With his drum, a little money he had saved, and a small knapsack of personal belongings, Orion made his way slowly southward, attaching himself to various newly organized troop units along the way. From Chicago to Springfield, past St. Louis and Cairo, and down the Mississippi River to Memphis, he was always able to find a regimental officer or chaplain who sympathized with his determination to join his father and brother and offered to help him on his journey.

When Orion, tired and dirty after the six-week trip, reached Memphis, he soon located the camp of the 55th Illinois. He wanted to surprise his father and brother. He was directed to the street in front of the regimental headquarters.

As he approached he could hear from afar a great clatter of rub-a-dubs of drums and the shrill notes of the screeching fifes.

Hiding behind a tree, he saw his father striding alongside the fife and drum corps, counting out the marching cadence.

In the second row, almost concealed by his big drum, was little Lyston.

As the group passed by, Orion darted from his hiding place and shouted to his father, "Hello, Dad, here I am!"

Unruffled, Principal Musician Howe never lost a beat and barked out the command to his charges, "Halt! At ease!" Lyston broke ranks and rushed to greet his brother. Mr. Howe joined them.

"Well, son," said Mr. Howe matter-of-factly, "I see you made it after all."

For a moment Orion resented his father's indifference. "But, father," he exclaimed, "you're not excited in the least! I surely thought you would be surprised to see me! I'm disappointed."

Then Mr. Howe and Lyston told Orion that his aunt and uncle had written of his leaving Waukegan. They had therefore been eagerly awaiting him for many days. "I was not worried at all, son," his father told him, "for I knew you would get here come hell or high water."

"Well, I made it!" exclaimed Orion, and he told them briefly of his adventures along the way. "And I have a surprise for you. I have learned to drum, and not too badly, either."

He demonstrated his skill in a few ruffles and some of the army calls. When he had finished he said, "Now, father, you will have no excuse for not letting me join up and be with you."

By a stroke of luck, the drummer of Company C had just been sent home on the sick list. Mr. Howe therefore recommended Orion as his replacement. This was in September, 1862, when the boy lacked three months of being fourteen years old.

On his enlistment form he gave his height as four feet eleven inches, his complexion light, eyes blue, hair brown, his occupation as "a boy."

The father and two sons were together in camp for four months. But in February of 1863 the War Department abolished the post of Principal Musician throughout the Army, for the corps of fifers and drummers, many of them adults, were by then considered frills in an army where every man was needed to bear arms. Only a few of the younger drummers were retained as noncombatants who were required to play the calls and to assist in caring for the wounded.

So Mr. Howe was free to go home if he wished. For a time he considered re-enlisting as a private. But he was worried about the farm. Since Lyston and Orion were together, he felt that they would be able to get along without him. With both boys in tears at the separation, he bade them good-by, was mustered out of the regiment and discharged from the army, returning to Waukegan.

Though in different companies, the two brothers were not far apart. The regiment was attached to the army commanded by General Ulysses S. Grant during the preliminary battles and skirmishes of the Vicksburg campaign.

Years later the regimental historian of the 55th Illinois wrote of them: *The little Howes, our infant drummers, drummed well, proved hardy, never seemed homesick, were treated as pets, and passed through battle after battle, and march after march, untouched by disease, unscathed by bullet and shell.*

Vicksburg, Mississippi, over two hundred miles south of Memphis, was the main Confederate fortress which barred the movement of Northern troops and supplies south to Union-occupied New Orleans and the Gulf of Mexico. Control of the Mississippi River was absolutely necessary for Union success in the West.

Accordingly, General Grant began a concentrated campaign by land and water to clear the river for navigation to the sea. Vicksburg was the key to this plan. The 55th Illinois Regiment arrived to the east of the heavily fortified town on May 17, 1863, to take part in the siege of Vicksburg, which was to continue for six weeks.

Here it was that Orion, when only about fourteen and a half years old, earned the Medal of Honor, and gained national fame so that the name Howe became known throughout the Northern states. It happened in this way.

The charge of the 55th upon a section of the Confederate breastworks circling Vicksburg began at two o'clock on the afternoon of the nineteenth of May.

The front line surged forward like a human wave, dashing over stumps and the tangled limbs of felled trees, struggling through deep gullies bristling with brush, and climbing the steep slopes of the ravines. All this was accomplished in the face of a roaring, whistling storm of shot and shell from the Confederates, who were solidly entrenched behind the parapets of Fort Hill, the most northern of the nine forts ringing the town.

When this first line of attackers reached a deep ditch which obstructed their progress, they were unable to advance farther lest they become targets in the open space beyond. The toll in dead and wounded had been heavy, and the few men remaining could only hide behind the protection of logs and branches.

The second line of soldiers was about a hundred feet back of the ditch. Because of the withering enemy fire they could not move forward to the aid of their trapped comrades, nor could they advance to the attack. They were halted for over two hours while the firing from the Confederate fort, instead of lessening, became hotter and hotter.

The trapped and immobilized Union men hugged the earth, meanwhile keeping up such a continuous barrage of returning gunfire that the supply of ammunition began to run low. Something must be done at once to replenish the supply, for at this position it was essential that the intense and steady fire continue.

Because of the unevenness of the ground as well as the obstructions, ammunition could be brought to the soldiers on the fighting line only by special messengers, and in such quantities as could be carried by hand through the quarter mile of fallen tree trunks, timber, and ridges in full range of the enemy's fire of musketry, grape and canister, shell and solid shot.

Their white handkerchiefs tied to their left arms to identify them as noncombatants, the musicians were in the rear assisting the wounded, their usual battle assignment. Colonel Oscar Malmborg ordered the sergeant major to go to the regimental ordnance wagon far to the rear, organize these drummers and fifers, and send them one by one to the besieged soldiers in the front line with supplies of cartridges taken from the heavy ammunition boxes.

A continuous stream of boys was soon moving back and forth with the precious but dangerous burdens.

Always before this May day Orion had remained in the rear during battles. But his eagerness to witness this attack had caused him to go to the front lines, and he was not with the other musicians. Colonel Malmborg had twice ordered him back so that he would be out of danger.

The lad had stopped in a ravine just to the rear of the fighting lines, there making several wounded men comfortable by giving them water while awaiting litter bearers who would take them to the field hospital behind the lines.

When a passing fellow drummer told Orion about the order to the musicians to serve as ammunition bearers, he collected the unused cartridges from the belts of the dead and wounded lying nearby.

Using his blouse as a sack, he carried the supply forward to the command post. Orion made several trips with his valuable burden of shells, all he could carry at a time. From time to time the enemy shot literally covered the ground, plowing it up with shot and shell as he ran for dear life.

Again and again he ran down across the ravine and up the steep opposite slope. The historian wrote after the war:

> We could see him nearly the whole way as he ran through what seemed like a hailstorm of canister and musket-balls. So thickly did these fall about him that each threw up its little puff of dust where it struck the dry hillside. Suddenly he dropped, and hearts sank, thinking his brief career ended. But he had only tripped over some obstacle. Often he stumbled, sometimes he fell prostrate, was quickly up again, and finally disappeared from us, climbing over the summit. As the boy sped away for the last time, Colonel Malmborg shouted to him, "Bring calibre fifty-four!"

The men's guns had become dirty and heated from the continuous firing, and the officers needed this smaller-sized ammunition instead of the regular fifty-seven caliber. Orion saluted the Colonel smartly and said, "All right, sir."

After the war he told in his own words what then happened:

> I had gotten about half way over the cleared place when I was struck in the right thigh, but kept on running and soon reached a ravine. My blood-filled boot was sloshing as though it was full of water, and I was getting dizzy.
>
> A skulker whom I met in the ravine helped me across and up the other side. I kept thinking, "Can I make it?" as the dizziness increased. I commenced to realize that I could not get back to the regiment. I think I began to cry as I climbed the hill with the bullets striking all around. But I went on up the hill, stopping every few feet on account of the dizziness.
>
> As I reached the crest and more level ground, I saw General Sherman standing a few yards to the left, watching the lines. I was about to pass him when the thought struck me that this was the man to get the ammunition to the front line, so I went up to him.
>
> "General Sherman!" I cried a little hysterically, "won't you please send some ammunition to my regiment? The men are all out and I'm hurt and don't believe I can go again."

"What regiment do you belong to, boy?"

"55th Illinois, sir."

"How close is our line to the enemy's works?"

"Right up to the ditch, sir. It's deep and they can't get across. Please send the ammunition."

"I'll do it. Are you hurt badly? Wait, and I'll send someone to help you to the hospital."

"Never mind me. Send the ammunition!"

I turned away, and had limped five or six rods when I remembered about the size. I turned and called back, "General Sherman!"

He looked at me, and I literally screamed, "Send calibre fifty-four!"

He waved his hand so that he understood and I found the hospital.

Although the fifty-four-caliber cartridges never reached the soldiers and the attack was successfully repulsed by the Confederates, the pluck and fortitude of the boy drummer made an inspiring story which was included in all the dispatches and reports. General Sherman himself repeated the tale many times, and his version was printed in hundreds of newspapers, adding a touch of human interest to the glory of the fall of Vicksburg on the Fourth of July.

Orion's fame was even further increased when a poem entitled "Before Vicksburg—May 19, 1863," by George Boker, was published in the *Atlantic Monthly*. Little Orion Howe and his cry "Caliber fifty-four, sir!" thus became known to every Northern schoolboy, for many a patriotic program was climaxed by the stirring recitation of this narrative of his exploit.

The young hero was given a thirty-day furlough home to recover from his thigh wound. All Waukegan knew of the Howe boys, and General Grant himself, had he visited the town, would not have received a more tumultuous welcome.

Orion's veteran father did not even attempt to conceal his justifiable pride in his elder son.

Although the Medal of Honor was not awarded to Drummer Howe until many years later, in 1896, General Sherman did not forget him. In August, 1863, the General wrote to Secretary of War Stanton recommending Orion's appointment to the United States Naval Academy for training as a midshipman. He was too young to enter West Point, and the minimum age at the Naval Academy was less than eighteen.

*I'll warrant the boy has in him the elements of a man,* the famed commander wrote, *and commend him to the Government as one worthy the fostering care of some of its national institutions.*

Official red tape delayed the appointment. After a month in Waukegan, Orion returned to his regiment, his heroic act at Vicksburg being recognized by his promotion to Corporal on Christmas Day, 1863. This was also a birthday present, for Orion became fifteen four days later.

The two Howe brothers were finally separated when, on General Sherman's recommendation, Brigadier General Giles E. Smith appointed Orion as his personal orderly and courier. General Smith commanded one of the corps in Sherman's army. Lyston remained with the 55th Illinois Regiment, taking part in Sherman's March to the Sea, and was finally discharged in February, 1865, when he was only fourteen and a half years old.

On the route from Chattanooga southward through the state of Georgia, Orion was continuously under fire as he delivered messages to the various division and regimental commanders of Smith's corps. The young courier received an official citation as being "very useful" in the Battle of Resaca on the fourteenth of May. A fortnight later at Dallas he was wounded three times—twice in the right arm and once in the breast. These wounds disabled him so that his military career was interrupted.

He was in the hospital only a short time when the long-awaited letter from the Secretary of the Navy arrived in response to General Sherman's recommendation. Orion received permission to take the entrance examination of the Naval Academy, which was to be given at Newport, Rhode Island, in July. The Academy had been moved there from Annapolis for the duration of the war.

Given a sixty-day furlough to recover from his wounds, Orion went to New York City, where he studied night and day for a month, occasionally reporting to a local army hospital for medical care.

When Orion visited Newport in July he learned some of the details of the examination. As a farm boy in civilian life his schooling had been limited, and for the past twenty-one months as a soldier he had, of course, been given no opportunity to continue his education.

Confessing that he was entirely unprepared to pass the entrance examination successfully, Orion asked for a postponement. The Superintendent was impressed with the young applicant's appearance and enthusiasm and consented to defer the examination for one year so that he could catch up in his studies.

Orion returned to Georgia only long enough to say good-by to his brother, collect his possessions, and apply for his discharge from the army. In September he began tutoring with a Professor Botts in New York City, with whom he lived. His muster-out was dated the first of October.

So eager was he to take up the career of a naval officer that he studied long hours, practically memorizing the textbooks which had been given him. This was more difficult for Orion than for most seventeen-year-olds because he had not gone to school for over three years. But the next July he passed the entrance examination, not with the highest marks but with a better than average grade.

He became a cadet midshipman during the summer of 1865, but soon began having difficulties in keeping up in his studies. Due to his youth and lack of formal schooling, he was unable to pass the required courses, and he left the Naval Academy at the end of his second year, in June, 1867.

The call of the sea had become strong, however, and since he could not join the United States Navy, Orion became a sailor in the merchant marine, surviving the wreck of the bark *Thornton* in a severe storm off the coast of Ireland in November.

The pioneer West now attracted him. For the next two decades Orion Howe led a roving life as a cowboy and Indian fighter on the plains. He was a member of the Powder River Expedition against the Cheyenne Indians in 1876, barely escaping capture and scalping. Taking advantage of his wide experience with horses, he was for some years a saddle- and harness-maker. Finally he changed to the practice of dentistry in Buffalo, New York. By 1914 his wounds and sudden blindness had made him totally disabled. He died in 1930 at the age of eighty-two.

When his Medal of Honor was awarded him in 1896, thirty-three years after his Vicksburg exploit, the required recommendation of the surviving fellow-soldiers of the 55th Illinois Regiment stated that *he had showed rare presence of mind and strong nerve. His youth, his wounds, and his still continued adherence to duty at that time, demand special recognition.*

With the exception of Arthur MacArthur, Jr. (Chapter 13), fourteen-year-old Orion Howe was by all odds the most famous of the teenagers who won the Medal of Honor.

# CHAPTER 5

## *A Brave Bugler*

GWYNNE, NATHANIEL McL. Private, Troop H, 13th Ohio Cavalry.

For act of bravery at Petersburg, Virginia, 30 July 1864 (when he was exactly fifteen years old).

Citation: "When about entering upon the charge, this soldier, then but fifteen years of age, was cautioned not to go in, as he had not yet been mustered. He indignantly protested and participated in the charge, his left arm being crushed by a shell and amputated soon thereafter."

Born Urbana, Ohio, 5 July 1849.

Mustered in, 10 May 1864 (retroactive on 3 January 1865); mustered out, 21 March 1865.

Award made on 27 January 1865.

☆ ☆ ☆

THE buglers were to the cavalry what the drummers were to the infantry. Just as the drummer was called "the tongue of the camp," so the bugler was the "tongue of the horsemen," regulating the life of these mobile soldiers.

The routine calls of the cavalry in camp followed much the same schedule as those of the infantry drummers. The first call at five o'clock in the morning was "reveille," then "assembly" or roll call, followed by "breakfast call" at six, "surgeon's call" at seven, "drill" at eight, "recall" at eleven, and "dinner" at noon.

The buglers then rested, practiced, or performed their special duties as orderlies until four o'clock, when the second "drill" call was blown, with another "recall" at five, followed by "guard mounting" at half-past.

The call for "dress parade" at six-thirty was the most important of the day, for it was the signal for all the cavalry-men to assemble in lines, mounted and saddled, for the inspection ceremony. As in the infantry, "tattoo" sounded at nine o'clock was the signal for the final roll call of the day.

"Lights out" closed the day half an hour later. General Dan Butterfield's "Taps," composed in mid-1862, soon became the substitute for "lights out," though it was not officially adopted by the army for all branches of the service until 1874. "Taps" also became the standard notes to be blown on the bugle at military burials.

"Boots and saddles," one of the most used calls, was the signal for mounted drill or any mounted formation. This plus "the General" was used as the order to break camp—packing up, striking tents, and loading the wagons preparatory to marching, whether on foot or on horseback.

The cavalry bugle calls outnumbered those of the infantry drums because of the additional signals for the care of the horses. These often numbered more than a score daily, such as the "stable call" and "water call."

When on the move, the bugler's notes sounded along the line for the "trot," "gallop," and "charge."

A cavalry troop on special duty, called a horse detachment, used its bugler constantly, whereas a drummer rarely accompanied an infantry company when it was sent out as a scouting party or as a unit of skirmishers. In such a roving assignment where a group was constantly on the move, a drummer would not only have difficulty in keeping up with the men, but would be useless, for the sound of the drumbeat would reveal the location or presence of the unit.

On the other hand, the bugler was an absolute necessity to the roving bands of cavalrymen who might become widely scattered when on patrol duty. Only the bugle notes, blown loud and clear, could be heard above the sound of the horses' hoofbeats, the clatter of their shoes, and their neighing. At the sound of "reassemble," the dispersed cavalrymen would be able to determine the location of the leader and, guided by the calls, gather together again.

When a part of a separated cavalry detachment unexpectedly came upon the enemy, the notes of the bugle would summon the others to its aid or rescue.

As has already been noted, few cavalry buglers were teenagers, for the rugged life of the horsemen was too strenuous for most of them. Only one boy bugler, Nathaniel Gwynne of the 13th Ohio Cavalry, earned the Medal of Honor during the Civil War, though twenty or thirty older cavalry buglers performed acts which won them the Medal. Gwynne's award was unique among buglers, for his troop served as dismounted cavalry because horses were not available to them at the time.

"Nat" Gwynne's grandfather, Thomas Gwynne, the patriarch of the family, started west from Maryland in 1826. While stopping off in Pennsylvania, he and his family were converted to the teachings of Emmanuel Swedenborg and joined the Swedenborgian Church of the New Jerusalem. Mr. Gwynne became a lay preacher, finally settling in Urbana, Ohio, in the 1840's. This was in the southwestern part of the state, north of Cincinnati and Dayton.

His two sons, David and Thomas, established a stove factory there. When Nathaniel was born on the fifth of July, 1849, his father (David) was already a prominent citizen of the town and of Champaign County. At that time

Mr. Gwynne had just been made president of the first County Board of Education.

As the most prominent local members of the Church of the New Jerusalem, Nathaniel's father and his uncle Thomas founded Urbana University (Swedenborgian) in 1850. During the 1850's the firm of David and T. M. Gwynne changed to the manufacture of steam engines, then a pioneer industry. Their model won the first prize in mechanics at the Ohio State Fair in 1854.

However, the success of the Gwynne steam cooperage firm came to an end with its failure in the panic of 1857. Undaunted and "with God's response to our prayers," the brothers were able to salvage enough assets to organize the first private bank in the county.

Champaign County proved not wholly in sympathy with the Civil War, for its citizens possessed a heritage of Abolitionism alongside a hatred of war. When the war came, these two ideas were often in conflict.

In the prewar decade many stations of the Underground Railroad were scattered throughout its communities, for runaway slaves crossed the Ohio River at Cincinnati and moved directly north through the county on their way to Canada. Abolitionist feeling was high and Champaign County was the scene of many incidents involving fugitive slaves.

As the war continued into 1863, the antiwar elements became particularly strong in that section of Ohio. Copperhead sentiment (opposition to the war) grew by leaps and bounds in Champaign County, for Clement Vallandigham, the most outspoken opponent of the war, was a resident of Dayton, in the next county south.

His views were widely supported in southern Ohio. His pro-Southern opposition to Northern participation led to his arrest, military trial for disloyalty and treason, and banishment beyond the federal lines in the month of May.

Because the sentiments of his family were strongly against all war, Nat Gwynne could not even mention his desire to become a soldier. When he could no longer endure the family opposition, he ran away in the spring of 1864, making his way south to Cincinnati, where Ohio regiments were regularly being organized at Camp Chase.

When the recruiting officer looked at Nat, who was not yet fifteen (he lacked two months of being that age), he shook his head and said, "You had better stay at home, my boy. You're too young."

But the lad was not at all disheartened by the rebuff. He had broken with his family. To return would mean humiliation and possible punishment. He *must* therefore find some officer who would accept him.

The 13th Ohio Volunteer Cavalry was in camp, and its rolls were almost filled. Nat hunted up several of the officers and begged that he be allowed to go with them. He appealed to the captains of each troop (the designation of companies in the cavalry). Those of A, B, C, D, E, F, and G refused to listen to his plea. He followed them in alphabetical order.

There remained only Troops H, I, and K, for the letter "J" was not used as a designation because of its similarity to "I." He was becoming increasingly disheartened when he interviewed First Lieutenant William Mark, commanding Troop H. The officer was so favorably impressed with Nat's sincere desire to serve his country that he made him an offer.

"It's entirely against the regulations for me to accept you," he told the youth. "The recruiting officer of the regiment has refused to enroll you, and you know that I cannot go over his head. But I believe you have the makings of a good cavalryman. Perhaps if you came along with my boys and proved that you deserved to be mustered in, we can work it out, in spite of your being underage. How would that be?"

"How would that be? Absolutely perfect," responded the

eager lad. "And I promise that I'll be such a good soldier that they'll forget my age! When do we leave?"

So it was that Nat Gwynne was in line when the men of Troop H were sworn into the service of the United States. But when the entire regiment was mustered in on May 3, his name was not heard on the first roll call of the troop as Union soldiers. In all else, however, he was "Private" Nathaniel Gwynne and was to become a true soldier.

A blow awaited the 13th Ohio Cavalry when it arrived at Washington a week later. The men were told that they were not immediately to be given horses and cavalry arms but would act as infantry soldiers—dismounted cavalry—for sixty days. Most of the men had enlisted expecting to be horsemen. Their morale dropped to a low level, and they were understandably disgruntled.

To make matters worse, their first experience as foot soldiers was, to say the least, disheartening. The regiment was sent to Virginia, and after disembarking at White House Landing on the James River, marched hours on end, in rain and mud, in pitch-black darkness. The soldiers covered sixteen miles one day, seventeen the next. When he had been in the army exactly a month, Nat had his baptism of fire at the second battle of Cold Harbor on June 3. He was so overjoyed to be "with" the army, though not yet "in" it, that it mattered little whether he was an infantryman or a cavalryman. It was enough to be an unmustered soldier.

The regiment crossed the Chickahominy River on the sixteenth and bivouacked near Petersburg, where the Army of the Potomac was laying siege to this Confederate stronghold which protected Richmond from attack from the south. Petersburg was surrounded by a vast and intricate network of trenches, breastworks, and fortifications.

For more than a month the men of the 13th Cavalry were idle, for a stalemate had developed. The lines of both the

Blue and the Gray were ominously silent, as if waiting for
a signal to action.

"Private" Gwynne had been given a trumpet and had
become proficient in all the calls. He played only those
required for the infantry in camp, for the regiment was still
acting as dismounted cavalry and none of the special signals
were needed.

During this period of inactivity one of the most daring
and ingenious engineering feats of the entire war was being
completed within two miles of the 13th Cavalry.

This was the famous Petersburg mine. The idea came
from Lieutenant Colonel Henry Pleasants of the 48th Pennsylvania Infantry. A mining engineer before the war, he
obtained the approval of General Burnside, and eventually
of General Grant, to dig a tunnel extending under the Confederate artillery battery at a key point in their fortifications.

The tunnel was to run 511 feet to a point 20 feet below
the battery, with two lateral galleries, of a total length of
75 feet, under the enemy trenches. A powder charge of 8,000
pounds (320 kegs) was to be placed under the Confederate
works.

Most of the soldiers of Pleasants' regiment were Pennsylvania coal miners. They began digging on June 25 and
finished on July 25. The tunnel averaged five feet in height,
was four and a half feet wide at the bottom and about
two feet wide at the top.

All the dirt had to be removed by hand in hardtack boxes,
and the pickaxes had to be muffled so that the Confederates
would not discover the scheme. In spite of the precautions,
however, the Southerners were aware of the construction
work going on under their fortifications. They were able to
make preparations to counter the explosion when and where
it might take place along the lines.

Plans had meanwhile been formulated for an assault to
be launched through a gap made by the mine blast. At first

Negro troops were to have been used, but the idea was abandoned because previous encounters between Negroes and Confederates had resulted in Southern outrage. The top Union commander, General Burnside, substituted a division of white soldiers, but he failed to prepare passages through his parapets and obstructions to make it easier for the attacking forces.

On the day after the mine was completed and the fuses laid, the 13th Ohio Cavalry, one of the regiments in the division chosen to make the assault, moved forward to trenches within a hundred yards of the Confederate lines. For the next three days they were briefed on the part they were to play in the attack.

The regimental historian described the tense situation on the fateful morning:

> About three o'clock on the morning of the thirtieth, we were marched a little to the right and there, massed on a low piece of ground, were many thousands of boys in line of battle with bayonets fixed for the charge. We were ordered in line. With bayonets fixed and guns at half cock, we lay flat on the ground. We knew the mine was to be exploded at 3:30.

The fuse, however, failed to work. At 4:45 A.M., after repairs had been made, the mine exploded. The blast created a crater over two hundred feet long, sixty to eighty feet wide, and twenty to thirty feet deep. At least 275 Confederates were at once killed or wounded; nine companies of South Carolina regiments were blown into the air. The historian continued:

> We were lying about seventy-five feet east of the rebel fort, just inside our line. A few minutes after sunrise the earth rose under us several inches, it seemed, then receded again. Looking to the west, we saw an immense volume of smoke and dirt mingled with men, cannon, small arms, boards, camp equipage

of every kind, ascending into the air a hundred feet or more. Some of our own men were dazed by the blast.

The sergeant of Troop F also vividly described the immediate effects of the explosion:

> Just about sunrise, a trembling of the earth was felt, and a dull roar was heard. I looked to the front and saw a huge column of dirt, dust, smoke, and flame of fire apparently two hundred feet high, which curled like a plume. In the air I could see in the column of fire and smoke the bodies of men, arms and legs, pieces of timber, and a gun carriage.

For fifteen minutes thereafter about a hundred cannon and fifty mortar guns poured shot and shell mercilessly into the Confederate breastworks. During this terrific bombardment the Southerners almost miraculously recovered from the first stunning effects of the explosion and began to return the Union fire with an effective artillery bombardment.

In the followup Union attack, Nat Gwynne disobeyed orders and won the Medal of Honor.

Just as the 13th Ohio was about to make the charge with the division about half an hour after the explosion, the captain of Troop H noticed Gwynne in line and shouted to him, "Young man, remember you are not mustered in. You had better stay behind. That's an order."

"But that's not what I'm here for!" responded the boy. "I came to fight and fight I will!"

Just then the regiment's chief bugler sounded the "charge," which they understood as well as if they had been mounted. Away on the run went the troop, young Gwynne swept along with it, across a ravine, up a hill, straight to the mouths of the waiting enemy cannon.

Shell, grape, and musket balls swept the field between the breastworks and the crater, and three out of four of the Union soldiers in the division were struck down. Nat rushed on, almost oblivious of the men falling all around him.

When the men reached the crater, they plunged straight into it like sheep instead of surrounding it. Within its hollow they were ordered to lie down. The scene within the gaping hole was one of unbelievable confusion: *The bottom of the pit was filled with bodies and parts of bodies, boards, artillery wheels, broken caissons, pieces of iron. Many of the Confederates wounded in the explosion were half buried, attempting to free themselves.*

The soldiers of the first regiments to arrive were deep in the crater, battling hand to hand with Southern soldiers and falling from the shots of sharpshooters. Gwynne and his fellow soldiers were near the edge, however, and were not trapped. When they were ordered to emerge, Confederates were awaiting them. Each soldier chose the nearest of his adversaries, attacking him with bayonets and clubbing him with muskets. Bayoneted guns were pitched back and forth like harpoons. The soldiers even used clods of the loosened earth as weapons. This was truly a struggle to the death.

In this encounter the color sergeant of the 13th was shot down and the regimental flag captured. The enemy had proved too strong for the Northerners. The attack had failed, and the order "Retreat!" was given.

The Union soldiers began running back from the crater to their own lines. Bullets kept drumming and humming, zipping and whizzing. When half the distance to safety was covered, Nat Gwynne suddenly and impulsively turned around and retraced the path of retreat. Heedless of the shower of bullets, he made directly for the Confederate line.

The captor of the 13th Ohio's flag was holding the banner, drooping on its staff amid the smoke of battle. With super-human strength Nat felled the surprised soldier with a blow on the jaw, clubbed him with his musket, seized the precious banner, and started back toward his own lines.

Immediately every gun of the enemy was trained on him. He had not gone far, however, before the arm holding the flagstaff was shot away, almost tearing it from its socket, and he dropped the flag. But with his other hand Nat picked up the emblem and continued his dash toward the Union lines.

Again he was hit, this time in the leg below the knee, but he was able to crawl the rest of the distance. When he reached the safety of the Union trenches and handed the flag to his comrades, he fell unconscious to the ground.

The retreat was completed shortly after noon. The mine explosion had been a success, but the follow-up was a failure. The casualties were huge, the total one of the worst of the war for an eight-hours' fight.

"Private" Gwynne's short army service was finished. He had fought in two major battles and had been so seriously wounded that his arm had to be amputated. He had never been mustered into the army.

While he was recuperating from the amputation at the General Hospital in Alexandria, Virginia, his troop commander wrote the War Department citing Nat's act at Petersburg and asking that he be mustered into the army dating back to the May day when he had taken the oath with the regiment at Cincinnati.

At that time Brigadier General John Slough of Ohio wrote: *I have known him from infancy and can testify to his patriotism and courage. He is a bright and intelligent boy and his chief regret appears to be that the loss of his arm will render him unfit for further military service to his country.*

The fact that a soldier had taken part in a military action, and, what was worse, had been wounded, when he was not yet officially a soldier, appeared to shock the War Department bureaucracy. Such a situation was unheard of. They could not acknowledge such an error.

But some unnamed official was moved to recommend Nat Gwynne for the Medal of Honor and to urge that he be officially mustered in on the third of January, 1865, effective retroactively to the tenth of May, 1864, when he had "entered" the service.

Nat was still in a Cincinnati hospital early in February when both the medal and his official certificate of enrollment reached him. He was now belatedly an acknowledged Private in Troop H of 13th Ohio Cavalry.

Veteran Gwynne, mustered out of the service on the twenty-first of March when not yet seventeen years old, was given funds to purchase an artificial limb. He studied law and ultimately began to practice in Missouri. He married in 1873, and a son, Daniel, was born the next year.

The stump of his left arm, in which he had carried the flag of the 13th Cavalry and had held the bugle while he regulated the life of his fellow soldiers in Troop H, gave him a great deal of trouble, for the nerves had been injured. His knee wound caused him to limp for the rest of his comparatively short life.

He was a familiar figure in Grand Army of the Republic parades, when he was able to appear as a true cavalryman with saddle, boots, and spurs, an honor which had been denied him in the army.

Death came to Nathaniel Gwynne on the sixth of January, 1883, when he was only thirty-four years old. In the funeral procession at Kansas City, his gray horse followed the hearse, bearing the empty saddle of its former rider, the unmustered cavalryman, as well as his bugle, boots, and spurs.

"Nat" Gwynne, the heroic boy bugler, had truly embodied the "soldier-like qualities" required of those who win the Medal of Honor.

# CHAPTER 6

## *The Gunner*

COOK, JOHN. Bugler, Battery B, 4th United States
Artillery.

For act of bravery at Antietam, Maryland, 17 September
1862 (when he was fifteen years and one month old).

Citation: "Volunteered at the age of 15 years to act as a
cannoneer, and as such volunteer served a gun under the
terrific fire of the enemy."

Born Cincinnati, Ohio, 10 August 1847.

Mustered in, 7 June 1861; mustered out, 7 June 1864.

Award made on 30 June 1894.

☆ ☆ ☆

THE buglers of the artillery regiments were "the tongue
of the gunners." Their calls were almost identical with those
of the cavalry, except for the additional signals involving
the movement and manning of the light and heavy guns.

Like the cavalry, the artillery units were highly mobile,
for they were moved from place to place as needed. The
various batteries (the artillery designation for companies)
of a regiment were often assigned far from one another,
serving independently. Few of the field batteries remained
for long in one spot.

The horsedrawn guns were dispatched wherever battles
were anticipated, for the artillery supported the infantry,

softening the enemy with bombardment and covering the foot soldiers in their attacks with protective fire.

Even in battles the artillery often did not remain in a fixed position. At the high tide of action orders would arrive for a battery to transfer quickly to another part of the field.

The horses would be harnessed to the guns and caissons (ammunition wagons), the cannoneers and gunners would take their places, one on each horse, the others on the gun carriages, and the unit would rush under fire to the new position.

In all these situations the bugler was called upon to blow the calls many times while the guns were firing.

Some of the artillery units were mounted, and the bugler, riding on horseback next to the troop commander, sounded the additional calls regulating its speed of movement.

The only teenage artillery bugler to win the Medal of Honor was a member not of a state regiment, but of a Regular Army unit. He was John Cook of the 4th United States Artillery.

The regiment, founded in 1821, had a proud history of engagements in Black Hawk, Seminole, and Mexican Wars. When the Civil War broke out, the 4th was scouting and fighting Indians on the western plains. Like many other Regular Army units, it was recalled for duty in the East and brought up to full strength. New members were signed up in the principal recruiting centers. Battery B's new enlistees came mainly from Ohio.

John Cook, from Cincinnati, lacked two months of being fourteen years old when he signed up as Battery B's bugler, in June, 1861. The Battery was a mounted light artillery unit of 150 officers and enlisted men, with six guns, a dozen caissons, and a limber for each.

The guns were Napoleon twelve-pounders (howitzers), so called from the weight of the solid ball they fired. The bronze Napoleons weighed 1,250 pounds and were called "the artillery workhorses of the Civil War."

After spending a year in the defense of Washington, Battery B was assigned to the Army of the Potomac and began its participation in a long series of actions which continued until one week before the end of the war. These ranged from relatively minor engagements where a single battery or only a few of its guns were used to major battles where hundreds of heavy and light artillery pieces were in action.

After the Battle of Cedar Mountain in September, 1862, Bugler Cook was made orderly to Lieutenant James Stewart, the commander of one of the two-gun sections (a six-gun battery had three sections of two guns each). Thereafter in battles he would ride along the line with the Lieutenant or would dash to a distant gun emplacement bearing orders for firing.

One of the members of the Battery remembered the young bugler:

> Johnnie rode a bob-tailed pony, which we always hated to see in the line of battle because she made a center target for the enemy's shells. Sometimes Stewart would send him to the rear, in order to get the pony out of sight of the enemy. "Get that damn ghost out of sight!" the officer would yell sometimes, when the enemy would begin to reach for little John and his white pony with their shells.

Immediately after the second Battle of Bull Run, the 4th moved north into Maryland, and after South Mountain was in the "bloodiest day of the war" at Antietam, on September 17. This was where little Johnnie Cook—he was not even five feet tall—distinguished himself.

General John Gibbon, the brigade commander, received an order to advance to the front and attack. He ordered Stewart's section to set up its guns in a grass field between two straw stacks.

Beyond this field within the range of the guns was the cornfield which was to become so famous. As the infantry soldiers pushed forward, the guns fired over their heads.

Finally the two field pieces of the section were moved to the front. One gun was placed on the pike, the other in the field nearby. Gibbon ordered the other two sections of four guns under Captain Joseph Campbell to the left. Johnnie Cook was temporarily assigned to the Captain as courier to co-ordinate the sections.

Just as Lieutenant Stewart's section was unlimbering (setting up its guns) preparatory to shelling the woods beyond, a column of Confederate infantry emerged and poured a rain of shells into the unprotected group of Union men. Within a matter of minutes two dozen of the Battery were killed or wounded, the latter being quickly carried to the shelter of the two straw stacks.

At this time the bloodiest part of the battle was going on in the cornfield directly to the left. General Gibbon wrote of it in his memoirs:

We knew little of what was going on beyond our immediate vicinity. We were in the hottest of hornet's nests and had all we could do to attend to what was in our front while the sounds of severe battles reached our ears from all directions.

Bullets, shot, and shell whistled and screamed around us, wounded men came to the rear in large numbers, and the six guns of Battery B hurled forth destruction as the enemy increased in numbers, rushed forward to capture the guns.... The enemy came so close to the Battery in the desperate attempts to capture it, that the Napoleon guns were double-shotted with canister before whole ranks went down, and dead men were piled on top of each other.

Captain Campbell on his horse galloped from gun to gun of his sections, Johnnie Cook at his side. The sergeant of the Battery had been severely hurt when one of the guns had run over him in its recoil.

Just as the Captain dismounted to help with the gun, his little roan pony Pompey, simultaneously struck by seven bullets in the body and a shell bursting in her mouth, fell dead.

Campbell was hit twice, one of the bullets tearing his shoulder, which bled profusely. He was too weak to walk to the rear where he could receive medical attention.

Johnnie dismounted, ran to the Captain, lifted him up, and stumbled with him to the rear, turning him over to an ambulance driver. Campbell ordered the boy to report to Lieutenant Stewart immediately and tell him to take command of the Battery.

The young orderly quickly returned to the firing line and delivered the message. The dead and wounded of the Battery were lying near their guns. Two were unmanned and silent, the other four understaffed and firing only sporadically.

Johnnie sprang from his horse, unstrapped a pouch of powder from the body of a dead gunner who was lying near one of the caissons, ran forward with it, and "served" the gun until the end of the fight.

A gun was ordinarily manned or "served" (the term for the steps leading to its discharge) by a crew. A sponger cleaned the vent with grease, a rammer pushed in the shell and the powder charge, a cannoneer primed the gun, and a gunner sighted for distance and trajectory (curve of the shell when shot). Another jerked the lanyard (cord) at the command "Fire!"

At this point in the fierce battle, Johnnie performed all the functions—he was sponger, rammer, cannoneer, and gunner. While he was feverishly serving the Napoleon, someone handed him a shell. Johnnie hesitated only long enough before ramming it into the vent to see that the soldier who had come to his aid was wearing the single gold star of a Brigadier General on his shoulder.

Somewhat modestly, Cook wrote of this experience:

> We were then in the very vortex of the battle. The enemy had
> made three desperate attempts to capture us and the last time they
> came within ten or fifteen feet of our guns. It was at this time
> that General Gibbon rode up, and seeing me struggling alone with
> my gun, jumped from his horse, and in the full uniform of a
> Brigadier General, worked as a gunner and cannoneer with me.
> He was very conspicuous, and it is indeed surprising that he came
> away alive.

This was certainly a unique combination, undoubtedly not
duplicated in the War—the full Brigadier General and a
fifteen-year-old boy serving a gun together.

The fire of the five double-shotted Napoleons finally beat
off the enemy. Battery B lost thirty-nine men killed and
wounded, and about thirty-three horses.

In recommending his bugler for the Medal of Honor
nearly thirty-two years later, Lieutenant Stewart testified,
"His courage and conduct in that battle was the admiration
of all who witnessed it."

But Johnnie Cook was to see a great deal more action.
After Antietam he crossed the Rappahannock River in the
December assault at Fredericksburg and was under heavy
fire at Chancellorsville in May, 1863.

Battery B was in action in all the three days of the Battle
of Gettysburg. Lieutenant Stewart had replaced Campbell
in command as a Captain. He used Johnnie as his mounted
orderly. Throughout the battle the boy rode under the direct
aim of the enemy riflemen. Back and forth he galloped,
carrying messages to and from the section stationed on the
left, nearly half a mile away.

When the losses were very great and the Confederates
were closing in, Captain Stewart, who had been wounded,
ordered the guns and caissons of the Battery on Cemetery

Hill removed out of the line of fire. One of the caissons, with its axle broken and four of the horses which drew it killed, was abandoned.

Cook dismounted, ran back to the wagon, prepared a fuse and lit it, destroying the ammunition to prevent its being captured and used by the enemy. Stewart cited this act as well as the action at Antietam in recommending Johnnie for a Medal of Honor.

Johnnie Cook's next battles were in the Wilderness during May, 1864, then at Spotsylvania Court House, North Anna, and finally Bethesda Church. By that time he had almost completed his three-year term of enlistment. Bethesda Church on June 2 was his last battle.

The regimental historian paid a tribute to the young soldier in this situation:

It was at least his twentieth battle, and he was still less than seventeen years old. Literally, Johnnie had more battles than his years. His time was out, he had his honorable discharge in his pocket, and was only awaiting transportation to go home.

But his bugle never sounded so loud and clear as it did when he followed the Captain and blew "Forward, trot!" and "Forward, gallop!" as our horses stretched their necks out for that rebel battery on the pike!

The Captain did not want Johnnie to go into action on that day. Maybe he had a superstition that a man or boy who went into a fight when his time was out would be killed. But Johnnie had got that old scent of powder up his nose once more, and nothing could stop him.

So away he went, following the Old Man along the pike and blowing his bugle as lustily as ever, while the enemy's canister cut down the brush by the side of the road or screamed over our heads. And when we finally limbered our guns and made them "talk," Johnnie was everywhere as usual, riding back and forth along the line of battle, as fresh and eager as if he were a tenderfoot rather than a veteran!

Like many another youthful soldier, John Cook at the end of the War disappeared into the anonymity of civilian life. The only postwar official record of him was the award of his Medal of Honor in 1894. The record shows that he was still alive in 1897, and that his son John also served in the Regular Army in the war in the Philippines.

The exploit which earned for John Cook the Medal of Honor was almost without parallel in the annals of the Civil War. It was truly unique for one boy to exhibit such mature judgment, such skill in serving the guns, and such complete lack of fear.

He more than met the qualifications for the Medal of Honor as one of the soldiers "who shall most distinguish themselves by their gallantry in action."

CHAPTER 7

# A Youthful Commander

MURPHY, ROBINSON E. B. Musician, Company A, 127th Illinois Infantry.

For act of bravery at Atlanta, Georgia, 28 July 1864 (when he was fifteen years and two months old).

Citation: "Being orderly to the brigade commander, he voluntarily led two regiments as reinforcements into the line of battle, where he had his horse shot out from under him."

Born Oswego, Illinois, 11 May 1849.

Mustered in, 6 August 1862; mustered out, 2 June 1865.

Award made on 22 July 1890.

THE 1861 recruits for the Union Army were organized and outfitted by the states, and offered to the federal government by the governors, who vied with one another for the honor of exceeding the quotas which had been assigned to them.

Companies were recruited locally, then sent to regional camps to be absorbed into the regiments being organized there. As a result, several companies might be enrolled from the same county, and the members of a single company (between eighty and a hundred men) might all be from a single town or township.

Every community, large or small, held "war meetings" at which prominent citizens and local military figures urged the able-bodied men to enlist. These speakers used every possible argument which might prove effective—appeals to manhood, patriotism, bravery, and the defense of family and fireside.

The best orators put forth these various motives with all the persuasive powers at their command. After their speeches, the volunteers came forward to the recruiting officer's desk and signed the register of enlistees amid the cheers of admiring friends, neighbors, and relatives.

In the country towns these meetings were held in the town hall or square or a schoolhouse. A regular speaker at these gatherings in the little village of Oswego, Kendall County, Illinois, in the northern part of the state southwest of Chicago, was Wright Murphy, a local lawyer and public-spirited citizen.

During the early months of the war his eloquence and sincerity influenced many men to enlist. So convincing were his arguments and appeals that his twelve-year-old son, Robinson, whose nickname was Bob, became determined to join up.

Mr. Murphy refused to grant Bob the necessary permission, saying that his place was at home and in the classroom, not on the battlefield or in a camp with older and experienced soldiers.

Bob's strong feeling about the necessity for preserving the Union sprang from the many stories he had heard of his ancestors and their fight for freedom in the French and Indian and Revolutionary wars. In the former his great-grandfather and great-uncle had been killed and scalped by the Indians, as were ten small children with them.

Others of his forefathers had fought under General Anthony Wayne at Ticonderoga and were members of the first colonial regiment commanded by General George Washington. Young as he was, this heritage of fighting for liberty would not permit Bob to be only an observer in this newest struggle.

The seed of determination had been planted in the boy's mind, and Bob took matters into his own hands. He knew that regiments were being mustered into the army at Joliet, Illinois, eighteen miles away. So early in June he ran away from home, walking the entire distance across the country-side.

By great good fortune he made friends with several offi-cers of the 20th Illinois Regiment. One of them promised to take Bob with him when the unit left the camp ten days later. But Mr. Murphy had heard where Bob was, and the day before the scheduled departure he sent a friend to Joliet to bring his son back home to Oswego. So ended the boy's first attempt to become a soldier.

Very soon thereafter a recruiting officer from Chicago, who was making the rounds of Kendall County seeking vol-unteers, promised Bob that he would take him to Chicago and find a place for him as a drummer.

But when the officer was awaiting Bob at the appointed meeting place, Mr. Murphy arrived in place of his son and told the recruiter that his son, who had been locked in his room, had changed his mind about enlisting. This was the end of Bob's second attempt to go to war.

For many long months the restless lad was closely watched by his alert father. He could not figure out a plan of escape because he would be recognized before he had gone very far from home. By now everyone knew that lawyer Murphy's son had been twice thwarted in his attempts to enlist, and furthermore they knew that his father continued to refuse his permission. So Bob reluctantly continued his schooling.

In the summer of 1862, at a war meeting held at the County Court House in Oswego, Mr. Murphy as usual was called upon for a speech. This time he was more than ordinarily eloquent and persuasive. He ended his remarks by saying, "I have asked a great many men to enlist. Now I propose to enlist myself."

At this, Bob jumped up and went forward to put his name on the list beneath that of his father. But Mr. Murphy pulled him away. "I've told you many times, son," he said a bit wearily, "that you are too young. You still are. Besides, you are my only son and you must stay at home with your mother. I shall soon be going away for three years."

This did not satisfy the youth. Repeated arguments took place in the Murphy home during the next fortnight. The father used every possible objection he could think of, but his words, as before, went in one ear and out the other as Bob pretended to listen out of respect for his father.

Finally the boy took a long breath and said, simply and quietly, "Papa, if you don't consent to let me go with you, I will run away as soon as you leave. I will join some other regiment and we may never see each other again. I do not want to be disobedient, but I *am* going to war."

As a lawyer, his father realized that his arguments were no longer effective. He reluctantly gave his consent. Bob was enlisted as the drummer of Company A, 127th Illinois Infantry Regiment, on the fifth of August, 1862, when he was thirteen years and three months old. His height was recorded as four feet six inches, his occupation as "schoolboy."

Mr. Murphy, a private in the same company, was fifty-one years old, well over the maximum age limit of forty-five. The regiment was mustered into the United States service at Camp Douglas in Chicago in September of that second year of the Civil War.

Father and son went off to war together. Bob soon became an expert drummer. For almost two years the 127th Illinois wandered far and wide, first being sent to Tennessee, then south into Mississippi, where it participated in the siege of Vicksburg. From there it went west to Arkansas, helping to capture Little Rock.

For more than a year Bob was orderly to the Colonel of the regiment in addition to being Company A's drummer. He was faithful and efficient in his duties, so much so that the Colonel recommended him to become orderly to General Joseph A. Lightburn, then commanding a brigade of the Union Army's XVth Corps.

In January of 1864, Bob reluctantly parted from his father and fellow Illinois soldiers, starting for southeastern Tennessee to assume his new duties.

But while en route the train on which he was riding collided with another, and Bob suffered a severely wrenched back. On a surgeon's certificate that he "was unable to move," he obtained a thirty-day furlough home. The stay with his mother in Oswego aided his rapid recuperation.

Back in the Army, as General Lightburn's right-hand "man," the young orderly rode far and wide on a fine bay mare delivering messages and orders among the many units of Lightburn's brigade in the Army of the Tennessee. The whole army was moving south into Georgia on the long and arduous campaign toward the objective of Atlanta.

Bob was under fire during many of the successive hard-fought battles along the route. He became personally acquainted with most of Sherman's generals, including Logan of his home state, Howard, Hooker, McPherson, Dodge, Blair, and Schofield. They all called him by his nickname of Bob. No "Robinson" for them!

Certainly he was one of the few fifteen-year-olds in the Union Army—he reached that age in May just as the campaign began—who was familiar with the military strategy on the topmost level and acquainted with the command responsibilities of the officers of the lower ranks.

Bob Murphy was often present with General Lightburn when important decisions were made. Many times he pored over maps marked with the plans of attack. The lessons he learned were in many respects the equivalent of the training given prospective officers at the United States Military Academy at West Point.

The young orderly absorbed this information like a sponge, and was able to use it in July, when he was given command responsibilities which led to his award of the Medal of Honor.

By July 22 the advance units of the Union Army had reached the outskirts of Atlanta. The Confederate resistance under Generals Hood and Wheeler had resulted in an enormous toll in killed and wounded. But after Kenesaw Mountain and Peachtree Creek, Sherman poised his eager troops for a mortal blow which would penetrate the Southerners' ring of defenses around the city.

The twenty-second of July of 1864 was a sad day for the soldiers of the Army of the Tennessee, for on this date their beloved commander, Major General James McPherson, was killed. The fighting in front of Atlanta on that day had been particularly violent. The enemy charged again and again, and one of the Union divisions was forced to change its front seven times in the afternoon.

During this fighting, General McPherson, advancing alone, rode into an ambuscade of Confederates. Recognizing the rare target of a General, they took careful aim and shot him dead. He fell from his horse. Under continued gunfire his aides quickly rescued his body and removed it well within the Union lines.

General Lightburn, with Bob as orderly at his side, viewed the body before it was taken away in an ambulance. In the reshuffle of the command, Lightburn was put in charge of a division and General John Logan became Commander of the Army of the Tennessee.

At the Battle of Ezra Chapel to the west of Atlanta on July 28, General Lightburn's division, including the 127th

Illinois Infantry Regiment, was on the extreme right of the main forces of the Army of the Tennessee and being flanked by the enemy.

The rebel onslaught was terrific, and their line of battle enveloped the 127th Illinois, threatening to cut it off from the rest of the Union forces.

From his vantage point with General Lightburn, Bob could clearly see what was happening. He realized that his father and his friends, the soldiers he knew so well, were in a desperate position. He cried out to the General, "My father is in there! What can we do? We *must* save him!"

Above the din of battle General Lightburn shouted, "Bob, go over to the main line, find General Logan, and see what he can do to save us!"

Young Murphy rode his pony wildly down the line to where General Logan was watching the battle. With tears in his eyes he told "Black Jack," "The rebels are cutting our right all to pieces and we must have reinforcements if we are to be saved!"

The commander calmly replied, "I know all about it, Bob. I've already ordered reinforcements from the left. Here they come now! If you know exactly where they are most needed, show 'em in!"

Bob Murphy, then only two months over fifteen years old, knew exactly what to do. So he quickly rode to meet the Colonel commanding the two approaching relief Ohio regiments, and yelled, "Follow me!"

At first the officer did not understand that this stripling had been authorized to assume command. But Bob shouted, "I come from General Logan and I know what must be done at once!" The officer lost no time in giving the command, "Forward! Line up! Charge behind this lad!" to his men.

The cheering soldiers advanced on the double-quick to the threatened points, re-forming the lines and driving the enemy back over the hill toward Atlanta.

In the charge Bob's horse was shot out from under him, but he continued going forward on foot. Though soldiers fell all around him, he urged them on, running at the side of the color-bearer. The assault was successful. The casualties were many, but the day had been saved.

Bob was a true hero. General Lightburn later wrote that he was *not only a brave and faithful soldier, but displayed a remarkable judgment for one of his age, as I soon found out.* In a pension affidavit many years later, the General added, *He served as my orderly and was conspicuous for his bravery and for intelligence and promptness in obeying orders.*

As a reward for his skillful and successful leadership, Bob was given a furlough the next month to return home on a sad mission. His father, by then fifty-three years old, had endured the rigors of army life and been under fire many times, but was now broken in health.

As they started back, Bob knew that he was taking his father home to die. The elder Murphy passed away soon after their arrival in Oswego, and the son was able to comfort his mother during the remainder of his sixty-day leave.

Atlanta had already fallen when Bob returned to duty. The boy was reassigned as orderly to General Joseph Webster, Sherman's Chief of Staff. He accompanied the officer in the March to the Sea.

The war was soon over! Bob's last army experience was when he rode in the Grand Review of the Armies in Washington on the twenty-third of May, 1865. When he was discharged in the capital ten days later, Robinson Murphy, though just sixteen years old, was a veteran of two years and ten months of service.

Still a young man with the war behind him, Mr. Murphy became a salesman, traveling from Chicago into the deep South as far as Galveston, Texas. On one of his many trips he met his future wife, whom he married in Mobile, Alabama, in 1875. To the young couple were born two daughters in addition to a son who died in infancy.

After his retirement in 1918 he lived with a married daughter until his death in 1934 at the ripe age of eighty-five. He was buried in Arlington National Cemetery.

Only full colonels commanded regiments during the Civil War, so Robinson E. B. Murphy was undoubtedly the youngest soldier, and certainly the only private, to lead not one but two regiments in an attack. His Medal of Honor act was therefore one of the most unusual of all those for which awards were made.

# CHAPTER 8

# The Courageous Brothers

THOMPSON, JAMES and ALLEN. Privates, Company K, 4th New York Heavy Artillery.

For act of bravery at White Oak Road, Virginia, 1 April 1865 (when James was fifteen years and three months old, Allen seventeen and a half).

Citation: "Made a hazardous reconnaisance through timber and slashings, preceding the Union line of battle, signaling the troops and leading them through the obstructions."

James: Born Sandy Creek, New York, 25 December 1849. Mustered in, 15 February 1864; mustered out, 13 October 1865.

Allen: Born Sandy Creek, New York, 1 October 1847. Mustered in, 21 June 1863; mustered out, 26 September 1865.

Award made on 22 April 1896.

ONLY two sets of brothers received the Medal of Honor for Civil War service—John and William Black, brothers from Streator, Illinois, serving in the 37th Illinois Infantry, and James and Allen Thompson of the 4th New York Heavy Artillery.

The acts of the Blacks were performed separately at battles in Arkansas during 1862. But the Thompsons acted together as volunteers on the same mission.

The little village of Sandy Creek, New York, in Oswego County on the shores of Lake Ontario, was nothing but a crossroads when the Civil War began. The first physician in the township was Doctor James A. Thompson, who located at the settlement in 1815 and began a practice which was to continue for forty-four years.

Mr. Thompson was a typical country doctor of the time. He often rode over twenty miles on horseback to visit a patient and was well known and respected in the region. He became a father twice during middle age. Allen was born in 1847, James two years later on Christmas Day, 1849. The boys, then young teenagers, were left fatherless when Dr. Thompson died on the eve of the Civil War.

After the United States Congress had authorized and called for half a million volunteers in July, 1861, all of Oswego County was sending more than its quota of recruits to the Union Army.

Though only fourteen years old, Allen enlisted in the 81st New York Infantry at that time. Since he was almost six feet tall, he had no difficulty in convincing the recruiting officer that he was eighteen years old. His term of service was to be three years.

His service was short because he contracted measles on the way to Washington, and then bronchitis, which became so serious that he was hospitalized for four months and finally discharged for medical reasons in April of 1862.

But Allen was constant in his determination to be a soldier, so when companies of an artillery regiment were being organized in northern New York State in the midsummer of 1863, he again signed up as a private in Company K of the 4th New York Heavy Artillery. Again he was listed as eighteen, though he was actually only a month over fifteen and a half.

For seven months Private Thompson was on guard duty near the national capital. The life was easy, and he wrote home to his little brother James that his work as a soldier was pleasant and not too strenuous.

For a long time James had been planning to join his brother. Several cousins had become soldiers, and the boy felt left out of all the excitement and adventure which other members of the Thompson clan were experiencing. With the persistence of a teenager set on having his own way, he began pestering his mother for her permission to enlist.

Like thousands of other Northern mothers in the same situation, Mrs. Thompson attempted to dissuade him.

"Jim," she said, "you are now the man of the house. I need you here. Let the others add to the glory of the Thompson name. Besides, what can a little boy like you do in the army?"

"I can shoot, Mother, you know it. I'm one of the best hunters hereabouts. I want to shoot rebs instead of game."

"It sounds easy as you say it, Jim," his mother countered, "but you remember that your brother broke down under the hardships of that life even though he was older then than you are now."

"But, Mother, you know what he said in one of his letters. The life is easy and quite pleasant, and his health has never been better."

"Yes, yes, I know. But in this letter which just arrived he writes that the regiment is soon to go into action, which is quite a different matter."

But Jim continued his nagging. Finally Mrs. Thompson gave up the struggle, for the more she attempted to reason with him the more closed his mind became.

When she realized that the contest was a losing one, she said, "All right, Jim. I'm not going to give you my permission. That I can and will never do. But if you can be accepted on your own, I suppose I will have to accept your action.

Of course you will have my blessing and my prayers will follow you wherever you go. At least I will know that Allen will be taking care of you."

The Oswego County recruiting officers were apparently willing to overlook the fact that James was but two months over fourteen, and enrolled him as an eighteen-year-old private in Allen's company.

In the middle of February, 1864, he set off for Washington, proud and manly in his new uniform of blue. The great adventure had finally begun.

The 4th New York Heavy Artillery soon was in the fighting, continuing through all the Virginia campaigns until the end of the war at Appomattox more than a year later. James' ability as a crack shot proved useful. He often acted as an advanced skirmisher and protected the busy artillerymen as they manned the heavy guns. He and his brother never performed the duties of gunners or cannoneers; they were more like infantry soldiers.

The list of major battles in which the Thompson brothers took part for the next twelve months was a long one. By the final campaign in the last weeks of the war they were in the midst of the fighting when the Confederates were being driven west from Petersburg to the final surrender at Appomattox Court House.

The beleaguered Southerners had made a gallant stand to the west of the town, and so desperate was their defense that the Union Army had to gain ground by inches. It was in one of these heroic Confederate stands at White Oak Road that the Thompson brothers won their medals.

For three days the 4th New York, acting as infantry, had been in the line of battle, engaging in daily attacks upon the breastworks of the heavily entrenched Confederates.

On the morning of April 1 the regiment was advancing through the dense woods and underbrush in the line of battle.

They were feeling out the location and strength of the enemy.

After they had advanced about half a mile, they came upon a narrow slashing in the woods. Beyond this the Union soldiers could see the enemy breastworks clearly. The technical name for this type of fortification is an *abatis,* felled trees arranged so that their tops are turned toward the enemy to prevent his approach. A slashing forms a protective obstruction through which it is almost impossible for the enemy (in this case the Union soldiers) to advance in the face of the showers of bullets fired at short range.

The only way to get through this slashing was to form into columns of four, which would mean probable annihilation if a trap had been laid for them. Not a flag was in sight, not a rifle cracked to break the silence of the morning. It looked highly suspicious.

In the mind of every one of the New York men was the thought that perhaps an ambush awaited them. The deserted look of the Confederate breastworks was unnatural; the very silence seemed to call for caution. All eyes turned toward the plainly visible enemy fortifications. Every man was anxious to know the secret they concealed. So the regiment hesitated for twenty minutes while the Union officers assembled to work out a plan of action.

Soon the brigade commander, General Nelson Miles, came riding along the line. "What's wrong, Colonel?" he asked. "Why are you stopping? You're holding up the advance of the entire division."

The officer pointed out the narrow passage and its obstruction of trees. "Supposing, General, that it is a trap. It would be suicidal to send the troops there where they might be targets for the waiting enemy. We just can't do it!"

A first-rate General makes quick decisions, and Miles was that (he was a Medal of Honor winner). He realized that the officers would never order their men into this possible ambush. So he took over the situation, speaking to the soldiers themselves.

"Men," General Miles shouted, "you cannot stay here! You must move ahead. Who will volunteer to go through the timber and find out what is beyond it? How about it, boys?"

With five others, James and Allen Thompson stepped to the front. One of their friends protested. "Boys, think of your mother. You should not go together in such a dangerous place. Allen, you're the oldest. You go and leave Jim here in safety." But the protest fell on deaf ears, for the volunteers were already receiving instructions from the General.

The seven volunteer scouts were told to advance through the woods about fifty feet apart. They were to make their way as silently as possible through the underbrush and fallen timber, several on each side of the *abatis*, without being observed. They were to determine the position of the enemy and report back to General Miles, who would be waiting.

They were told to carry their rifles ready to fire the minute they came across an enemy soldier. If they saw the main Confederate force, one of them would climb a tree and wave his cap as a signal for the waiting troops to advance.

Moving forward together, Allen and James were far in advance of their companions. After penetrating the woods some two or three hundred yards, they ran upon a group of Confederates. The rebels leaped from the brush, covered the brothers with guns, and demanded their surrender.

In a flash the boys realized that if they threw down their arms and obeyed, no signal would reach their waiting fellow-soldiers. Not only would their mission be a failure, but most likely it would result in a disaster to their companions.

At once the brothers decided to die rather than surrender. Raising their rifles, they fired. Fifty Confederates returned their shot at close range. The other five scouts concealed in the slashing heard the shots and came to their aid.

During this encounter Allen climbed a tree with almost unbelievable speed and frantically waved his cap in the agreed signal. Below him the five other volunteers fell dead, killed almost instantly. James was able to escape their fate by lying low in the underbrush, covering himself over with branches and leaves and barely breathing. In the confusion he was not discovered.

Climbing down from the tree the instant he had given the signal, Allen ran back through the slashing to report to General Miles the details of what he had seen from the treetop. He was joined by his brother.

Word was quickly passed throughout the two Union divisions on the front line, and a successful charge was made, the two brothers leading the troops at the side of the Colonels. The 4th Regiment lost ninety men killed and wounded but captured that many prisoners and several guns.

The Confederates were eventually pressed beyond the captured breastworks. At dawn of the next day, April 2, the attack was renewed, continuing to Sutherland's Station on the following day. Here James was severely wounded. He had come safely through many battles, but his luck had run out about a week before the end of the War.

James Thompson spent six months in various Army hospitals, finally reaching Albany, New York. There he was discharged from the Army in October. He was only a little under sixteen, a seasoned veteran of twenty months' service. The war had by then been long over.

The act of the Thompson brothers eight days before Lee's surrender at Appomattox Court House was one of many during the final days of the war which were recognized by Medal of Honor awards. This was a period of continuous last-ditch stands by the Southerners, and these acts of bravery by Union soldiers undoubtedly hastened the war's conclusion.

Allen had been mustered out in September, but the military life appealed to him, and he re-enlisted in the Regular Army (4th United States Infantry) in March, 1866. During three years of service in the West he decided he wanted to settle there. After his discharge he therefore joined a wagon train and remained in Colorado and Wyoming as a rancher until his death in 1906.

James returned to Sandy Creek and spent the rest of his life there as a farmer, husband, and father of three children.

In 1896 each of the brothers was awarded a Medal of Honor, with identical citations. The honor was well deserved, for they had acted together voluntarily and "with disregard of personal safety."

# CHAPTER 9

## *"Jennie," the Drummer Boy*

LANGBEIN, J. C. JULIUS. Musician, Company B, 9th New York Infantry.

For act of bravery at Camden (South Mills), North Carolina, 19 April 1862 (when he was fifteen and a half years old).

Citation: "A drummer boy, 15 years of age, he voluntarily, and under a heavy fire, went to the aid of a wounded officer, procured medical assistance for him, and aided in carrying him to a place of safety."

Born Germany, 29 September 1846.

Mustered in, 4 May 1861; mustered out, 20 May 1863.

Award made on 7 January 1895.

TENS of thousands of foreign-born Northerners were in the Union Army. Many were members of families who emigrated from Europe during the troubled revolutions of the 1840's, and who were therefore lovers of freedom and democracy.

One of these former aliens who became Union Army soldiers, John Christopher Julius Langbein, was born on September 29, 1846, in the small hamlet of Tauberbischofsheim, near Heidelberg, Germany. His father was the local innkeeper. When the lad was only two years old, the Langbein family set off across the seas in the steerage and settled in the crowded slums of New York City's lower East Side.

Julius—he never used his other given names—was fourteen and a half when the Civil War began in 1861. Immediately after the first call for troops the city of New York was in a ferment of patriotism. During the last days of April Colonel Rush C. Hawkins, a Mexican War veteran, set up a number of offices to enroll soldiers for a regiment he was forming. The core of officers and men in the ranks of the various companies had been members of local military drill teams who wore colorful Zouave uniforms.

These were the first men in the state to volunteer their services as a unit. The regiment was to be known as the Hawkins Zouaves. The qualifications for enlistment were designed to attract recruits of a high caliber—good health was emphasized and the age limited to between eighteen and thirty-five instead of the usual forty-five-year-old maximum. In three days, three thousand men volunteered, and from these a thousand of the best were screened and accepted.

The headquarters of the regiment were at Castle Garden on the southern tip of Manhattan Island, and the recruits drilled seven hours daily in nearby Battery Park. With other boys Julius hung around the parade grounds and made friends with many of the soldiers. He soon attracted the attention of Lieutenant Thomas Bartholomew, for whom he ran errands and performed other minor chores.

"Why don't you come along to war with me?" the Lieutenant asked his young friend one day. "All you have to do is to obtain your mother's signature on this," he added, giving Julius a copy of the release form which a parent must sign before the Army would accept a recruit under the minimum enlistment age of eighteen.

Mrs. Langbein, by then a widow, refused even to consider giving her consent. Julius was now the man of the family. The records do not tell us whether his older brother George was still living at home. He was too young and too delicate for the rigors of army life. He might just as well stop begging. The subject was closed. The answer was "no." That was final.

Though disappointed, the would-be Zouave was still optimistic. To Lieutenant Bartholomew he sadly reported his mother's unwavering opposition. "Sir, no luck at all. She's dead set against my leaving."

His friend was sympathetic. "Perhaps if I talked with her ..." he suggested. They agreed that, rather than have a formal interview, Julius would ask his mother to invite the officer to dinner. The subject could then be introduced into the conversation casually.

On the appointed evening Julius was understandably nervous. His two younger sisters were captivated by the colorful Zouave uniform worn by the guest and his mother was cordial in her welcome. But no sooner had they sat down at the dinner table than Mrs. Langbein surprised them completely by bringing up the subject of Julius' enlistment.

"Lieutenant, I'm delighted to meet you after hearing so much about you. But don't think you and my son are fooling me. I'm quite aware that you two have cooked up a scheme and that your being here tonight has a definite purpose. I should warn you—and Julius knows it—that my decision is final. My mind is made up and you will just be wasting your breath in trying to change it."

But Lieutenant Bartholomew was not to be discouraged. "Mrs. Langbein," he said, "I can understand your sentiments. Julius has told me all your arguments, and they are natural to a loving mother. But he has been smitten with war fever and I should warn you that he will probably run away to join me when we leave for Virginia. Wouldn't you rather have him go with your permission?"

He continued to talk quietly and persuasively to her.

Julius would carry a drum instead of a gun. Musicians were forbidden to be in the thick of battle. Some soldier could carry Julius on his shoulder during long marches, or he could ride in the supply wagons. The outdoor life would be more healthful than the city streets, and he would become robust.

"Mrs. Langbein," he concluded earnestly, "suppose I promise to watch over him personally, keep him close to me, and write you regularly. Would you then accept my oath as an officer that your boy will be cared for?"

At long last the mother was convinced. "All right, Lieutenant, my son may go with you. However, I intend to hold you to your promise. Give me another release form and I will sign it. I threw away the one Julius brought home."

"And *I* rescued it from the wastebasket, Mother, and here it is! And here is pen and ink!" The lad smothered his mother with kisses and hugged her tightly. "Well, Julius," she exclaimed, laughing through her tears, "I can't fill in the information and sign my name if you don't let go of my arm!" The sisters cried, the mother cried, and Julius, try as he might not to break down, finally gave way to tears of joy and relief.

The very next morning, May 2, Julius Langbein enlisted as a drummer in Lieutenant Bartholomew's Company B of the 9th New York Volunteer Infantry, the official designation of the Hawkins Zouaves. Though actually fourteen years and seven months, his age was recorded as fifteen, in accordance with the policy of using the age at the nearest birthday.

The new soldier boy was immediately fitted with the colorful Zouave uniform—tasseled scarlet fez, short blue jacket and shirt embroidered in black, red silk sash tied at the waist, and loose baggy red trousers tucked into white gaiters. A magnificent new drum completed the outfit.

For the next month the raw recruit received daily instruction on the techniques of drumming, beating out the rhythms for the drilling squads for hours daily.

When on June 5 the regiment marched from their barracks (then at Riker's Island) to the East River pier where the S.S. *Marion Peabody* and *George Peabody* were docked, crowds packed the curbs along the line of march, waving flags and handkerchiefs. Twice during their march to the ships which were to carry them south the soldiers halted for the formal presentation and acceptance of flags which the local women had made.

Bursting with pride and resplendent in his colorful regalia, Musician Langbein marched alone in front of Company B, beating out the rhythm for the parade on the bright new drum he carried. Lost somewhere in the immense crowd were his mother and sisters, from whom he had already taken a tearful farewell.

The trip to Newport News, Virginia, was the first Julius had taken since the voyage from Europe when he was a baby. During the six months in the Virginia camp he readily adapted himself to army routines. With the drumsticks his guardian Lieutenant Bartholomew had given him, he practiced the various standard calls for hours on end.

True to his promise to the boy's mother, the officer kept the young soldier under his protection. Instead of being billeted with the other drummers of the regiment, Julius shared the tent of Company B's officers and ate in their mess.

Julius was small (five feet), with the blue eyes, blond hair, and rosy cheeks characteristic of German boys. His features were so feminine that he could easily have passed for a girl. In fact, he always took the part of the heroine in the productions of the regiment's Zouave Minstrel and Dramatic Club.

One of the characters he played was called Jennie, and the name immediately caught up with the whole regiment. After that, throughout his army service, Julius was never

known by any other name than "Jennie," except at roll call
and on the payroll. "Jennie" did not mean that Langbein
was effeminate, but was actually a good-natured compliment
for the excellent way he impersonated girls on stage.

Though not under actual fire, because he remained with
the other drummers helping the wounded, Jennie was a
spectator at the attack where the Zouaves earned their nickname of the "Charging Regiment" and gained fame throughout the Northern states.

To gain a foothold on the inland waters of North Carolina, a joint army-navy expedition set out from Newport
News early in February, 1862. Landing on Roanoke Island
on the seventh, the Zouaves used their unique method for
the charge, a plan which reduced casualties and permitted
them to advance long distances in a short time.

At the first puff of smoke from the enemy rifles, the
Zouaves would throw themselves flat on the ground, letting
the shots go over their heads. Then, before the enemy had
a chance to reload, they would charge at full speed with
fixed bayonets, yelling their distinctive battle cry "Zoo, zoo,
ZOO!" the first syllable of the word Zouave.

The 9th's next assignment was an expedition from Roanoke Island to the mainland, with the objective of destroying the Culpepper Locks at the southern end of the Dismal
Swamp Canal, the approach to Norfolk, Virginia.

Transports bearing the Zouaves and two other regiments
crossed Pamlico Sound, moved up the Pasaquotauk River,
disembarking near Elizabeth City, North Carolina, in the
pitch-black darkness of the morning of April 19. In a long,
circuitous route beneath the terrible heat of the scorching
sun and amid the constantly rising dust they marched north
to a rendezvous with two more regiments, covering thirty-
two miles by midafternoon.

The journey was made longer by the treachery of a Negro
guide who led them ten or twelve miles out of the way.

They paused only to execute him on the spot for his deception. The 9th finally met the other troops at three o'clock in the afternoon, just a mile south of the little village of South Mills, near Camden, North Carolina, about twenty-four miles from Norfolk. The Zouaves were exhausted from the march and the heat, and faint from lack of food and water.

Colonel Hawkins' reconnaissance showed the enemy to be less than a mile away, and he asked the men if they were willing to make a charge immediately. "I can't order you to go, boys," he said. "It's up to you." As the weary men formed in rows for an attack, the Confederates evidently spotted their red fezzes, for cannon balls and shells began whistling through the trees above their heads.

The files of Zouaves moved out into the field while, according to the regimental historian, *like a bunch of firecrackers the enemy's muskets commenced to crack till the whole bunch got going.* When the soldiers were within two hundred yards of the Confederate position, Colonel Hawkins gave the order, "Double-quick! Charge bayonets!" and the men rushed forward shouting their battle cry "Zoo, zoo, ZOO!"

The historian described this charge: *It was then as if some superhuman hand, capable of holding bushels of bullets in the palm were hurling them upon us. A storm of leaden and iron hail fell around us and pelted us. Every inch of the air seemed thick with whistling messengers of death.*

However, the style of charge favored by the 9th seemed to be well known to the foe, for when the Zouaves fell upon their faces to avoid the whistling hail of bullets ... *they directed their fire lower, which caused it to ricochet upon the plowed ground, cutting into the ranks of the attacking force like a scythe into grass.*

Under this direct fire, fourteen Zouaves were killed and nearly a hundred wounded before the regiment moved to the shelter of the woods on the right. Another regiment followed up the attack successfully, dislodging the enemy from their entrenchments.

Colonel Hawkins, two captains, and two lieutenants were wounded in the charge. One of these junior officers was Jennie's sponsor, Company B's Lieutenant Bartholomew, whose testimony years later concerning his young friend's actions won Jennie the Medal of Honor:

> It was during the charge that a shell exploded near me, a fragment of which struck me just above the right ear causing a concussion. I fell to the ground and my comrades passed over me. My first impression on being struck was that I had been clubbed with the butt of a musket. I lost consciousness almost immediately.
>
> How long I lay there I know not, but when I revived it was with a strange feeling. I could not open my eyes. I could not speak. I could not move or make any sign, but my sense of hearing was acute. I was being handled. Somebody was moving me. I recognized the voices of Doctor Humphrey, our regimental surgeon, and Jennie.

Lieutenant Bartholomew later learned what had happened. Jennie Langbein had no intention of looking out for his own safety. When the order to charge was given, he went with the regiment. As his friend fell wounded, Jennie rushed up to him through the rain of bullets and the din and smoke of battle, caught him as he was wandering about deliriously and aimlessly within range of the enemy fire, and managed to lead him to a comparatively quiet ditch in the rear. After giving the officer a drink from his canteen, Jennie left, but soon returned with Doctor Humphrey. The officer continues the story:

> I felt the doctor pushing his fingers into my wound. He felt in and around it, and I heard him tell Jennie that it was of no use, I was nearly dead, and that it would be useless to move me.

Jennie soon returned, accompanied by Charlie Wiley, the drum major, a big, strapping fellow. Together they managed to carry me to a house used as a hospital near the battlefield where I was placed upon a bed. Here I again lapsed into unconsciousness. How long I remained so I cannot tell, but when I revived I was in full possession of my senses. It was night and there were two or three other wounded men in the room with me.

Soon there was a commotion, and I was told that word had been received that the enemy had been met by strong reinforcements from Norfolk, that they had turned and were marching toward us, fifteen thousand strong, with every prospect of driving us from the field. Perhaps we would be taken prisoners. Under the circumstances a retreat had been ordered and the question was, what to do with the wounded.

We had no ambulance, but only two or three army wagons, and some of the wounded would have to be left behind. The surgeon gave me another examination, said it would be useless to move me. I would have to be left to the mercy of the enemy. Several of the officers and men of my regiment came and bade me a last farewell, and I resigned myself to my fate.

Almost as soon as my comrades had left the room, in came Jennie. I had not seen him for some time. I could not think that he had deserted me, but I could not help wondering about his absence.

He came quietly to my bedside and whispered, "Keep quiet, Lieutenant, you shall not be left behind. I have arranged it all." And he hurriedly left the room. I did keep quiet, for I trusted him fully. I heard a heavy army wagon stop at the door. Some comrades carried out the other wounded and I was left alone. Oh, the suspense of that moment! Would the wagon move on? Where was Jennie?

I suppose it was but a few moments, though it seemed an age. Jennie soon came, and with him were two other drummers who quietly but quickly took me from the bed. Before I could think how it was done, I was placed in the rear end of the wagon where there was hardly room to put a child. I was actually squeezed in just as the wagon started. I was nearly doubled up, my knees and body bent.

I have never asked Jennie how he concocted and carried out his scheme, but I know that he alone saved my life, and I can never repay him.

The eighteen men crowded into the springless open wagon in a heavy rainstorm completed the night-long trip on the rough country roads. At dawn they reached the waiting transports which took them back to Roanoke Island.

Lieutenant Bartholomew was hospitalized for almost two months, but his oft-repeated tale of Jennie's rescue of him spread throughout the regiment.

In recognition of his act, the lad was given a thirty-day furlough to New York City, where his mother was eagerly awaiting him. With him he carried a note from the commanding officer of Company B to her:

> Camp Reno, Roanoke Island, N.C.
> April 21, 1862
>
> Dear Mrs. Langbein:
>
> It is impossible for me to send your son home on a furlough without a word. I must say that as a boy he is good and as a soldier he is excellent. Beyond all things I must speak well of his bravery and attention to duty on the field. During the last battle he was at his post during the heaviest of fire, and behaved like a gallant little fellow. You should be proud of such a son, for we all are. With much respect, I am yours truly,
>
> G. A. C. Barnett
> 1st Lt., Commanding Co. B, 9th N.Y. Vols.

These complimentary remarks were written several months before the Medal of Honor was legislated by the United States Congress in July. Jennie's medal was not awarded to him until a third of a century later.

On his return to the regiment following his home leave, Jennie was again in several major battles. While the Zouaves were making a charge at the Battle of Antietam he had a horse shot out from under him, for he was a mounted orderly. At Fredericksburg in December his drum was riddled by bullets, and at Suffolk the tassel of his fez was shot away.

He was far from being the noncombatant drummer boy his mother had been promised by Lieutenant Bartholomew! He was mustered out of the service with the regiment at the expiration of its two-year service period on the twentieth of May, 1863.

A war veteran when not yet seventeen years old, Julius began thinking of his future. He returned to school for a year, but when he reached eighteen he wrote his former officers that he wanted to become a West Point cadet now that he was old enough to meet the minimum age requirement.

In addition to the recommendations of various officers of the 9th Regiment, Colonel Hawkins wrote a personal letter to Secretary of War Stanton, saying: *I consider this young man in the light of a natural soldier, full of the proper spirit, and a natural true soldierly pride and above all truthful and honest and faithful in the discharge of his duty. I am sure he will make a good soldier.*

General Ambrose Burnside, his top commander throughout Julius' military service, offered to take him to Washington to see Lincoln personally regarding the appointment to the Military Academy. But before the visit could be arranged the war was ended and within a matter of days the President was assassinated, thus possibly changing the entire course of the boy's life.

Mr. Langbein continued his schooling, studying law and becoming very prominent in New York legal and political circles. When only thirty-one years old he was elected to the New York State Legislature. After serving two terms as an Assemblyman he was elected Justice of the 7th Judicial District Court of the State of New York. He and his older brother George wrote treatises on district and municipal court law and practice which became standard works in their fields.

Jennie, as he was always affectionately known in veteran organizations, was prominent in the Grand Army of the Republic, and for several years he was Commander of the Medal of Honor Legion.

In commending his rescuer for the Medal in 1894, Lieutenant Bartholomew, then a resident of Bridgeport, Connecticut, wrote, *I can never repay him. I can only pray to God to bless and prosper him in this world.*

The officer's wish came true, for before Jennie's death in 1910 at the age of sixty-three, as Julius Langbein—Assemblyman, Justice, and lawyer—he reached a high and honored place in his profession.

# CHAPTER 10

## *The Soldier-Artist*

SCOTT, JULIAN A. Musician, Company E, 3rd Vermont Infantry.

For act of bravery at Lees Mills, Virginia, 16 April 1862 (when he was sixteen years and two months old).

Citation: "Crossed the creek under a terrific fire of musketry several times to assist in bringing off the wounded."

Born Johnson, Vermont, 15 February 1846.

Mustered in, 1 June 1861; mustered out, 28 April 1863.

Award made in February 1865.

THE news of the beginning of the Civil War spread quickly to every hamlet, village, and crossroads in the Northern states. Developments were followed avidly. The response of the New Englanders was particularly speedy.

This may have been because the forebears of most of the natives of those oldest of American states had fought in the Revolutionary War. The cry "Preserve the Union at any cost!" was therefore not a mere phrase, for the war aims of the Union Army had a definite meaning to them.

Even the tiniest villages of the New England states were therefore eager to make contributions of both men and money. Johnson, a small village in the extreme northwestern section of Vermont, was no exception. The inhabitants could look around them and see the largest peaks of the Green Mountains—Mount Mansfield, with its picturesque Smuggler's Notch, and Whiteface Mountain. Many of the Green Mountain Boys had fought in the French and Indian and Revolutionary wars.

Jonathan Scott, Jr., the grandfather of Julian Scott, had been a soldier in the Revolution. So it was natural that the youth, who was a little over fifteen years old when the Civil War began, was eager to become a soldier. At that time he was attending the Lamoille County Grammar School. Among his fellow students were the future Admiral George Dewey of Manila Bay fame and Alphonso Taft, the father of the future President and grandfather of Senator Robert Taft.

Julian's father, Charles Scott, evidently did not share his son's resolve to be a soldier, for the youth ran away to St. Johnsbury, forty-six miles from Johnson, and enlisted as a musician in Company E of the 3rd Vermont Infantry on the first of June, 1861. It is interesting to note that on this same day and place Willie Johnston's father (Chapter 2) joined the same regiment in Company B.

Young Scott was to be both drummer and fifer. He was recorded as being five feet four inches tall, with fair complexion, hazel eyes, and brown hair. He was sponsored by a Captain Blanchard of Johnson, who put down Julian's age as sixteen, though he was at the time only fifteen years and three months old.

The regiment, one of the first of the state to leave for the front, was fully equipped within six weeks, and left for Washington late in July, *with a brass band numbering twenty-four, and nine hundred men, an athletic, brawny-looking set of fellows, consisting of farmers, lumbermen, merchants, mechanics, and two hundred school teachers, all armed with new Enfield rifles, with a baggage train of seventeen wagons.*

For several months the 3rd Vermont guarded the Chain Bridge in Washington, the main link between the capital city and Virginia.

One of the soldiers of Company K, Private William Scott of Groton (not related to Julian), made the regiment famous at this time because he was the "sleeping sentinel," condemned to death by a court martial for falling asleep while on guard duty at the bridge. His last-minute pardon by President Lincoln made him one of the most noted privates in the Union Army.

When General McClellan undertook the ill-fated Peninsular Campaign in the spring of 1862, the 3rd Vermont became a part of the Army of the Potomac and journeyed south.

During these months of service Julian Scott began to develop his natural ability for sketching. His sketch pad was as valuable a part of his equipment as were drum, fife, canteen, and haversack. The boy's interest in art must have been due in part to the fact that his mother was a relative of the English artist Turner, famous for his seascapes.

The artist's eye of the youth spotted pictures in every phase of his army life. He eagerly filled the blank pages of his notebook with rough drawings of what he saw, with the intention of developing them into finished paintings when he was no longer a soldier. His models were his companions sketched from life, and these were later to form the basis of the paintings which were to bring him fame after he had received formal instruction.

After the month-long siege of Yorktown, the 3rd Vermont took part in the many engagements and battles of the Peninsular Campaign and the Seven Days' Battles before Richmond, where Willie Johnston, the drummer of Company D, was to distinguish himself (Chapter 2).

The first major battle of the campaign was at Lees Mills, Virginia, on April 16. The Confederates were strongly entrenched and their commander brought out the artillery and opened fire. At first the Northerners replied vigorously, but were forced to seek cover. Now was the time for the followup by an infantry charge.

The terrain over which the four companies of the 3rd Vermont—D, E, F, and K—were to advance was a series of ponds or morasses which had been formed by the damming up of sluggish Warwick Creek.

This charge was the first assault made by the Army of the Potomac on an entrenched line of the enemy. Because the "sleeping sentinel," Private William Scott, was killed in the advance, it was commemorated in a poem by Francis Janvier, which memorialized the young soldier's payment of his debt to Lincoln with his life:

> Then, louder than the roaring storm, pealed forth the stern
> command,
> 'Charge, soldiers, charge!' and, at the word, with shouts a
> fearless band,
> Two hundred heroes from Vermont, rushed onward through
> the flood,
> And upward, o'er the rising ground, they marked their way
> in blood!

The four companies burst out of the woods and ran to the bank of Warwick Creek. Unclasping their belts and holding their cartridges in one hand and their muskets in the other, they dashed through the waist-deep water and mud of the stream amid a shower of bullets from the enemy rifle pits, charged up the bank, and routed the enemy, who fled in panic to the fortifications.

With cheers the Vermonters started to follow the Confederates, but they were ordered back by the Captain who had been instructed to wait for reinforcements in case he was successful in gaining the first rifle pits. While the Union companies were waiting for the arrival of relief soldiers, the Southerners, reforming their lines with reinforcements, launched a counterattack.

To their dismay the Yanks discovered that in spite of their precautions in crossing the stream, much of their ammunition was water-soaked, ruined, and useless. Sharing with one another whatever dry cartridges were available, they held their ground and waited, hemmed in on three sides by a greatly superior force and showered by musketry and artillery at close range.

They were in this exposed position for thirty minutes while the Captain frantically dispatched three different messengers to the Colonel across the river for reinforcements or permission to retreat.

During this time enemy bullets mowed down many of the trapped Vermonters. From his protected position in the nearby woods where he was waiting to care for the wounded, Julian Scott watched his comrades drop one by one into the stagnant water. Some of the more seriously wounded were unable to move and could not muster the strength necessary to keep their heads above water.

Like many another noncombatant drummer boy during the Civil War battles, the young artist-musician disregarded the ordinary assignment. With a mounting feeling of helplessness, he watched the injured soldiers struggling in the water or attempting to crawl to the safety of the bank. Finally he could no longer bear the sight. He must aid these helpless men!

Unarmed and in the face of the terrific fire, Julian dashed from the woods through the smoky haze. The first helpless soldier he reached was a heavy man, but the youth was able to drag him to the shelter of the trees. The second, leaning against Julian, was able to walk. Again and again the boy waded into the stream to aid the first wounded man he came across.

Often he stepped upon the bodies of the dead submerged

in the water. The gunsmoke was so thick that he could not make out which of his comrades he was aiding. The bullets from the enemy sharpshooters on the rising bank sounded like hailstones as they struck the water.

Julian's strength seemed inexhaustible, and grew, rather than became less, with each rescue. Twice he carried heavy men on his shoulders as if they were only sacks of flour.

Nine times the young drummer rescued wounded soldiers and brought them to the place where the regimental surgeons were caring for the wounded.

By this time the Captain had received the long-awaited order to withdraw. Other soldiers brought the rest of the wounded to safety behind the Union lines. Of the nearly two hundred men who had made the heroic charge only a half returned unharmed.

Julian Scott's feat was recognized throughout the regiment. Later, when the law regarding the Medal of Honor was passed, he was to be honored for his devotion to his wounded comrades.

The young drummer continued to serve through the subsequent battles of the campaign, spending the summer, fall, and winter at the Harrison's Landing base.

He was selected to become orderly to the division commander, General William "Baldy" Smith, who lived in St. Albans, Vermont, not far from Scott's home town. Smith had sought to become acquainted with all the soldiers from his region of the state and had hunted up Julian after the Lees Mills exploit to offer him the post. He was also attracted to the lad because the boy had taken a Confederate soldier prisoner and brought him into camp amid the cheers of his fellow soldiers.

Early in 1863 Scott was wounded and successively sent to a number of hospitals, finally arriving at the Army General Hospital at David's Island in the harbor of New York City.

It was the custom of philanthropic women of the city to visit the various wards in an attempt to bring cheer to the wounded there. On one of these visits, a group of women were attracted to the corner bed where Julian lay. The blank pages of his sketchbook had long since been filled, so he amused himself by covering the walls near his bed with charcoal and chalk murals based on the sketches he had made in Virginia. These were "rough drawings of camp scenes."

The visitors recognized that Scott possessed a talent which should be encouraged. When they questioned him, he expressed his eagerness to become an artist. The main obstacle, he said, was that he was to be sent back to his regiment as soon as he was well. He still had many months of his three-year enlistment period to serve.

In addition, he told them, he was penniless and could not afford the training he would need. Without false humility, he explained that his only assets were his native ability, his ambition, and his youth.

One of the women impressed with the lad's talent was Mrs. Richard Busteed, wife of a New York City municipal judge. She interested her husband and several of his lawyer friends in the ailing soldier. One of them, Mr. Henry E. Clark, visited Julian to discover for himself if the reports were true. He examined all the sketches made in Virginia and was favorably impressed. He agreed to sponsor the youth's art studies.

Lawyer Clark then visited the chief surgeon of the hospital, outlining his plans for Julian's future and enlisting the doctor's aid in obtaining a medical discharge for his protégé. The intervention of the physician resulted in the boy's being mustered out during the last week of April, 1863. Scott was then only a little over seventeen.

Mr. Clark made Julian his ward. He intended to send the youth abroad for study, but the wartime was not good for travel. Besides, he felt that the boy should make more sketches for practice. An extensive portfolio of such charcoal drawings undertaken not informally, as in the past, but seriously, could be shown to European teachers under whom he might seek to study, and might influence them to accept him as a pupil.

So eager was his patron to give Julian this necessary experience that he obtained a special pass from the War Department permitting the embryo artist to tour the various battle sites with the New York representatives of the United States Sanitary Commission. This forerunner of the American Red Cross sent civilian observers throughout the Union Army to check on the welfare of the soldiers.

So it was that Julian Scott had the rare privilege of observing army life not from the viewpoint of the soldier but from that of a civilian artist. No longer need he snatch time from his demanding duties as drummer and orderly to make sketches and studies. This was now his full-time vocation, and he applied himself with eager enthusiasm, filling book after book with on-the-scene sketches which he would later develop into paintings after he had received professional instruction.

During these travels throughout the army with the Sanitary Commission representatives Scott was able to meet many high-echelon commanders and to make portrait sketches of them. These, too, he would put to good use later.

On one of his trips to the Virginia battlefields early in 1865, Mr. Clark, armed with a recommendation from General W. S. Hancock, Julian's top commander during the Peninsular Campaign and the Seven Days' Battles, visited the Secretary of War in Washington to apply for a Medal of Honor on Julian's behalf. His exploit had already been mentioned in official reports. Within a day the award was made, and Mr. Clark waited until the medal had been engraved, bringing it to Julian as a surprise.

Soon thereafter, while Scott was riding over the battle-field of Savage's Station, where he had been during the Seven Days' Battles in 1862, he lost the medal. After several months he was given a duplicate, which he never again wore, but kept safely in its case.

When the War ended, Julian enrolled as a student in the National Academy of Design in New York City, recognized at that time as one of the finest of American art schools. His particular forte was, of course, military subjects, then enjoying considerable postwar popularity.

One of his instructors was Emanuel Leutze, the famed painter of historic and patriotic subjects, whose masterpiece, known to every American schoolboy even today, was "Washington Crossing the Delaware." Leutze was impressed with the lad's talent, and when he returned to Berlin in 1867, he took Julian with him to continue his studies abroad.

Returning to New York in 1870 after two years of study, Scott, still under the patronage of Mr. Clark, opened a studio. Military paintings were more than ever in favor, and he obtained many commissions from historical societies, individuals, and military figures.

He began showing his canvases in the annual exhibitions of the National Academy, to which in 1871 he was elected an Associate, a signal honor for one so young. Soon after this, he married and moved to Plainfield, New Jersey, where he lived until his death many years later.

The catalogs of the Academy exhibitions indicate the scope of Scott's subjects. Most of his work was purchased or com-missioned by private collectors and only a few can be seen in art galleries and museums today. Some of the most noted were of huge dimensions, intended to be hung as showpieces. Through these paintings one can trace the artist's experiences as a soldier and his later travels as a civilian observer on the battlefield sites.

The descriptions of two of his most famous canvases indicate their subject matter, usually revealed by their descriptive titles.

In 1870 the Vermont Legislature honored him as a native son by authorizing him to *execute a historical painting illustrating the Vermont troops in action, in some noted battle of the late war, to be hung in the State House, in commemoration of the valor of our soldiers.*

The fee was to be five thousand dollars. After some discussion the chosen subject was the battle in which more of the Vermont troops were under fire than in any other engagement—the Battle of Cedar Creek in the Shenandoah Valley on the nineteenth of October, 1864 (see Chapter 11).

For three years Julian Scott worked on the massive (twenty by ten feet) canvas, visiting the scene of the battle twice in order that all details should be correct. He prepared more than two hundred sketches of soldiers and horses. Most of the officers in the painting were sketched from life.

The picture shows the famous Vermont Brigade during the final moments of the successful charge ordered by General Philip Sheridan on that eventful day. A critic hailed it by writing, *Mr. Scott has given prominence to the privates, who did the hard work, and has pictured the scene as it really was, a battle in earnest, full of elan, courage, and determination, but also full of glory and pomp and horror.*

When it was delivered to Montpelier and hung in the Executive Chamber late in 1874, "The Battle of Cedar Creek" had a specially designed oak frame. In each corner was a carved shield bearing the name of one of the great battles in which the Vermont Brigade won particular glory.

To reward Julian Scott for the extra work involved through the enlargement of the picture over the original plans, the Legislature voted an additional sum of four thousand dollars. The huge painting still occupies a place of honor in the State House, as a living memorial to the soldiers of a century ago and as a tribute to one of Vermont's finest artists, the underage drummer boy of the State's 3rd Regiment.

Another of his most noted paintings, "The Death of General Sedgwick," a six-by-nine-foot canvas, shows the scene at Spotsylvania, Virginia, on May 9, 1864, after the General had been mortally wounded by a Confederate sharpshooter. Surrounded by members of his staff sketched from life, the commander lies under the trees as a surgeon attends him. Drummer boys and stretcher bearers, overcome by grief, stand near by, and a unit of troops passes in the rear. This work hangs in the headquarters of the Plainfield Historical Society.

Four 1862 incidents are among the other subjects painted by Julian Scott—"The Rear Guard at White Oak Swamp," "Cavalry Charges at the Toll Gate Near Ashby's Gap, Virginia," "Hancock at the Battle of Williamsburg" (Scott had seen him there), and "The Antietam Cornfield." These were all based on sketches made on the spot during his service.

Subjects from 1864 sketches include "A Sortie—Petersburg," "Forming Under Fire," and "An Incident at the Battle of Hawes Shop, Virginia."

Many of his simpler paintings concern aspects of soldier life—"Escaped Prisoners Nearing the Union Lines," from a sketch made in the Shenandoah Valley in 1864, "Near the Outposts," "A Camp Raid," "Reserves Awaiting Orders," "The Rescue of the Color-Bearer," "The Drummer," "The Bugler," and "A Game of Freeze-Out."

"A Flag of Truce" pictures a cavalry officer and his bugler, mounted, who have advanced beyond the lines to a point where the signal asking for a truce could be seen. The bugler is waving a white handkerchief on a stick to attract the attention of the enemy.

Following the example of his teacher Leutze, Scott also used the American Revolution as a frequent subject, painting the Hamilton-Burr duel, the capture of Major André, the famed British spy, and other such incidents.

In 1890 Julian Scott was appointed special government agent to report on the conditions of the Moqui Indians in seven Arizona and nineteen New Mexico pueblos. He wrote a monograph on their life and customs, which he accompanied with scores of detailed drawings. He also painted portraits of individual squaws and braves.

During his three years' stay in the West, he was adopted by the Navajos, with all the Indian rites and mysteries, as one of the tribe. He gathered hundreds of curios which formed a magnificent collection, unique of its kind.

As a member of the Jersey Blues, he was given the honorary title of Colonel and for many years was known by that title. Death came to him in Plainfield on the Fourth of July, 1901.

Julian Scott's uniqueness among teenage Medal of Honor winners lies in the fact that his Army service, unlike that of most soldiers, contributed to his long postwar career as an artist and furnished the subject matter for most of his work.

# CHAPTER 11

## *A Cavalryman's Catch*

PARKS, HARRY JEREMIAH. Private, Troop A, 9th New York Cavalry.

For act of bravery at Cedar Creek, Virginia, 19 October 1864 (when he was sixteen years and eight months old).

Citation: "Capture of flag."

Born Orangeville, New York, 24 February 1848.

Mustered in, 10 February 1864; mustered out, 17 July 1865.

Award made on 26 October 1864.

THE regimental flag (see Chapter 12) was always to be protected to the death. Many instances are recorded in which Union Army units were punished because their flags had been captured by the opposing Confederates, this even though the loss invariably meant the killing or wounding of the color bearer and the entire color guard.

Federal regiments lost hundreds of flags during the war, even as they captured hundreds of Confederate colors. Each of the many Southern victories, particularly in the first two years of the war before Gettysburg, "the high tide of the Confederacy," meant the acquisition of at least a few banners of Union Army regiments.

Northerners were as proud of the Confederate flags taken

in combat as were the Southerners of their captured Union banners. The capture of Confederate battle flags accounted for the largest number of Medals of Honor awarded for Civil War exploits—more than three hundred, a fourth of the total.

Though most of the citations are short, either "Capture of flag" or "Capture of the flag of the ——— Infantry," they sometimes indicate the desperateness of the struggle, which often involved the killing of the flag's bearer or hand-to-hand combat with him. Behind these terse phrases lies many a hair-raising story.

The phrase "Capture of flag" in the award given to Harry Parks is somewhat unique in several particulars. Teenager Parks captured his flag and its bearer without a struggle, not even on a field of battle. But within the space of less than an hour, on the same mission, he seized three Confederate supply wagons, taking their two drivers prisoner. His booty was therefore threefold—a Confederate regimental flag, three enemy captives, and three wagons and their contents.

Harry Jeremiah Parks was only a little over thirteen years old when the events of early 1861 brought on the war. As it continued he became more restless. As a farm boy, he was an expert horseman, and the vision of himself as a dashing cavalryman performing daring acts, dueling on horseback with a gray-uniformed enemy, set his imagination on fire.

His father laughed heartily at the very idea of his son joining the army, vowing that not only would he refuse to grant the permission necessary but he would seek Harry out should he run away, as he constantly threatened.

By mid-1863 Mr. Parks' objections had strengthened his son's resolve. Being nearly six feet tall, the lad thought he could possibly pass for eighteen at a recruiting office. But at Warsaw, the town nearest the Orangeville farm where he lived, he was well known, and the recruiting officers who had come out from Buffalo laughed at him. Besides, the draft had begun and the Wyoming County quotas in the latest call had been more than met.

The only course left to Harry was to run away to where he was not known or would not be recognized. Yet he waited for several months because he had been strictly reared to honor and obey his father. In the struggle between filial duty and his overpowering urge to be a soldier, the former lost out.

Without leaving even a note, Harry set out on a snowy day in January, 1864, his destination being Buffalo, far enough away (about forty miles) to prevent his father from finding him and taking him home. There he failed to convince several different recruiting officers that he was eighteen.

But the idea of abandoning his purpose was out of the question. So he went northeast a little over twenty miles to Lockport, and there he met with success in passing as eighteen. This was the age he put down on his enlistment form as a private in Troop A of the 9th New York Cavalry on the tenth of February. He was then just sixteen years old.

To conceal his action from his father, Harry used only his middle name, Jeremiah, and as such he was listed on all the army records.

Stationed in Virginia since the early days of the war, the regiment had lost many of its men and badly needed replacements. Jerry joined the 9th while it was in winter camp on the Rapidan River. The regiment, under General Philip Sheridan, was soon in action in major battles where the cavalrymen added to their laurels in the Wilderness, Bethesda Church, and Cold Harbor. "Little Phil's" growing reputation was enhanced by his performances in these crucial battles.

Grant gave him a major assignment in August—to drive

the Confederates from the Shenandoah Valley of western Virginia.

Private Jeremiah Parks had the experience of being on horseback for hours on end in the Valley operations. For ten weeks he acted as a scout, a raider, and a fighter. To him came the glory for which he had so ardently wished only a few months before.

The Northern infantry and cavalry forces moved slowly southward in pursuit of the Southerners under General Jubal Early, winning victories at Winchester and Fisher's Hill.

In early October the Union forces began their systematic stripping of the Shenandoah Valley, which was so complete and thorough that Sheridan said, "A crow would have had to carry its rations if it had flown across the valley." The cavalry proved themselves particularly effective in this task. Young Parks boasted that he personally set several forage-filled barns and houses afire.

The 9th New York was in the division commanded by twenty-five-year-old General George Custer, a dashing horseman who gloried in a mounted clash. His horsemen would range over hill and dale, the men whooping and hollering as if the skirmishes and battles were only games. They were a foolhardy lot.

By the ninth of October the Confederate cavalry had been ignominiously whipped through the skillful movements, forays, and charges of their opposites in blue.

General Early was still undaunted by the reverses his troops had suffered in the Shenandoah Campaign. Though outnumbered almost two to one (thirty thousand to eighteen thousand), he had complete confidence in the capabilities of his men. He was convinced that in one final encounter, skillfully using all his infantry forces, he could defeat Sheridan's seemingly unbeatable Army of the Shenandoah.

The Southern commander chose a time when his commander opposite was absent on a two-day visit to Washington to discuss future campaigns with the Secretary of War. Perhaps Sheridan should not have relaxed his vigilance. But he was positive that the end of the Valley campaign was near and that the Confederates could easily be driven in disorder south out of the Shenandoah.

Events were soon to prove how inaccurately he had underestimated the unconquerable spirit of General Early.

The Confederate attack was launched at Cedar Creek on the morning of October 19. Time and again Early's brave soldiers struck at the various Union infantry divisions. One by one the Northern units were driven in confusion to the rear, breaking up in the shock of the concentrated enemy assaults. The victory of the Southerners seemed assured.

General Early then made a fatal mistake. He failed to pursue the retreating Union troops. His cavalry was almost nonexistent. To pursue the enemy he would have to rely on the infantry, and they had fought long and honorably. Instead of taking the offensive again he waited for the Northerners to abandon the area.

The Union lines had all been crushed, the infantry had been pushed back, and their camps had been taken. Flushed with victory, groups of the Confederate soldiers began plundering the deserted encampments, breaking ranks and leaving their stations to do so.

The only Northern force left untouched was the cavalry, numbering about seven thousand, with a few batteries of supporting artillery. Strangely enough, they had not been ordered into battle by the infantry commanders.

The horsemen now took the offensive, charging into the overconfident and scattered enemy. The earth trembled under their horses' hoofs. By thus diverting the attention of the Confederates, the disorganized Union infantry gained time to re-form their lines. Time was what was then needed the most.

On his way back from the capital city, General Sheridan

had dawdled along the route, spending the night of October 18 in Winchester, fourteen miles north of Cedar Creek, where his army was encamped.

At six o'clock in the morning of the nineteenth one of his staff officers awakened him to report that firing could be heard from the south. Thinking it only a minor skirmish, the General went back to sleep. But when his orderly told him that the noise was continuing, Sheridan arose, dressed, and mounted his horse Rienzi.

This was at nine o'clock. The steady roar of full-scale artillery fire from the south was now so tumultuous that he was convinced that his troops were engaged in what sounded like a major battle. This impression was strengthened by the behavior of the Winchester citizens, who laughed insolently, pointing to the south as he rode by.

Rienzi galloped furiously, his rider's apprehension increasing by the moment. As Sheridan reached a rise in the ground about five miles from Cedar Creek, according to his memoirs, he *saw the appalling spectacle of a panic-stricken army all passing to the rear in confusion, telling only too plainly that a disaster had occurred at the front.*

As the General arrived at his headquarters a short distance from the battlefield, he was briefed on the situation by his top officers. Sheridan quickly determined the course of action he would take. For an hour he issued command after command, setting the time for an afternoon counterattack.

Although he had been seen by only a few hundred soldiers, news of their commander's return spread through the ranks as if carried by the wind. Only a leader like Sheridan, who had the wholehearted devotion and confidence of his soldiers, could have achieved the magical transformation which took place.

To reassure them while their officers were carrying out his orders, General Sheridan, mounted on Rienzi, rode

among his men, through the entire area to which they had
been dispersed, shouting, "We are going to get back our
camps and our guns! I am with you! Rally 'round your
flags, men!"

According to one of the soldiers, his appearance "changed
a mob of dejected fugitives into a military force of frantically cheering men."

Under his personal command the revitalized troops
launched an offensive counterattack in midafternoon. This
was the decisive charge pictured in Julian Scott's painting
commissioned by the State of Vermont (see Chapter 10).
Sheridan's inspiring presence and superb leadership turned
what was a Union disaster into a smashing victory.

The story of Sheridan's dash from Winchester became
one of the most celebrated incidents of the entire war. Rienzi
became by all odds the most famous and beloved horse in
the Union Army, just as Traveler, Robert E. Lee's mount,
was the favorite of Confederates.

A Pennsylvania poet-artist, Thomas Buchanan Read, was
in Cincinnati a fortnight after the Battle of Cedar Creek.
His brother-in-law saw a drawing of Sheridan and Rienzi
by Thomas Nast, artist and war correspondent, on the
cover of *Harper's Weekly,* and said, "Buck, there is a poem
in that picture." Read read the descriptive account of the
ride. There *was* a poem in the drawing, and within four
hours Read had written it.

"Sheridan's Ride" excited the imagination of all who
heard or read it. Little did it matter that the author was
incorrect in the distance from Winchester to Cedar Creek,
fixing it as twenty instead of fourteen miles. Each stanza
covered five miles of the ride, and ended with the reduced
distance to Cedar Creek—twenty in Winchester, then fifteen, ten, and five before the climax.

A selection of verses will indicate why Thomas Buchanan

Read's "Sheridan's Ride" was one of the two or three best-loved and oft-repeated of Civil War poems.

The first stanza sets the scene:

Up from the South, at break of day
Bringing to Winchester fresh dismay
The affrighted air with a shudder bore,
Like a herald in haste, to the chieftain's door,
The terrible grumble, and rumble, and roar,
Telling the battle was on once more.
    With Sheridan twenty miles away.

The second verse described the General's increasing un-easiness, the next the frantic beginning of the ride, ending at fifteen miles from the field of battle. Rienzi's "tail of a comet" to the ten-mile mark is next. Then

Under his spurning feet, the road
Like an arrowy Alpine river flowed,
And the landscape sped away behind
Like an ocean flying before the wind;
And the steed, like a bark fed with furnace ire,
Swept on, with his wild eyes dull of fire;
But, lo! he is nearing his heart's desire;
He is snuffing the smoke of the roaring fray,
    With Sheridan only five miles away.

The troops saw Rienzi and his rider coming, and the next verse describes Sheridan's arrival and his steed's seem-ing pride:

With foam and with dust the black charger was gray;
By the flash of his eye, and the red nostril's play,
He seemed to the whole great army to say:
"I have brought you Sheridan all the way
    From Winchester down to save the day."

The final verse is a paean of praise for Rienzi and his rider.

The Confederate rout was complete, and the surviving soldiers fled in a mass. The main pike was cluttered with artillery field pieces, caissons, supply wagons, and ambulances attempting to escape in the darkness.

Sheridan had not forgotten his pride and joy, the cavalry. He now gave them the assignment of pursuing the fleeing enemy southward and recapturing the materiel which had been taken in the morning. All of Sheridan's twenty-four guns were recovered, together with twenty-five Confederate field pieces, sixteen hundred rifles, fifty wagons, sixty-five ambulances, and over a thousand prisoners.

The horsemen in blue plunged into their assignment with gusto. Private Parks more than did his share, not once but twice, and in so doing earned the Medal of Honor.

Troop A became separated from the main body of cavalry, and each man was on his own. In his enthusiasm to do his share, Jerry galloped far in advance of his comrades. Before he realized it, he was in the midst of a very large body of Confederate soldiers. Darkness, however, shielded him from being recognized.

His own story shows how he preserved his presence of mind and extricated himself from the potentially dangerous situation:

I pushed on rapidly and presently came upon a Confederate who was carrying a stand of colors over his shoulder and an overcoat on his arm.

"Halt!" I exclaimed. "I want your flag!"

The rebel made a quick jump behind my horse, drew his revolver, shot once in the darkness, then made a dash for the creek nearby.

I wheeled my horse, pulled my own gun, and fired at him. I

must have scared him badly, for he threw up his hands in despair and shouted, "I surrender! Don't shoot again!"

And now the prisoner and the flag were mine. I marched the Johnny at the side of my horse till some time later, when I met one of our men, to whom I turned over my prisoner.

I advanced on the gallop still farther, and encountered two teamsters in charge of three wagons. I stopped and ordered them to "Turn around quick! Drive the other way! Follow me!"

In the darkness they mistook me for one of their own men and obeyed my directions without hesitation. I led them into our own lines and within safe distance disarmed them and brought them in as prisoners.

The wagons contained loads of choice eatables, cigars, and tobacco, and for several days our boys lived high and in luxury.

Eight other cavalrymen had captured enemy flags, two, as in Parks' case, not identified in the records. The others were of Georgia, North Carolina, and Virginia regiments. One of these soldiers had matched Jerry's record by taking a flag with three officers and an ambulance with its mule and driver.

As the cavalry moved north up the Valley on the next day, the nine men headed the mounted column. Each flag was carried by its captor, and, flying in the breeze, they raised the spirits of the exhausted men.

Soon after, Parks received an order to appear at General Sheridan's headquarters. He was to go to Washington with General Custer, the eight other flag captors, and a Vermont cavalry corporal who had taken Confederate General Stephen Ramseur, his personal flag, and the ambulance (and its driver) in which the wounded commander was being carried. The ten soldiers were to report to Secretary of War Stanton with their flags.

The group arrived in Washington early on the morning of the twenty-fourth of October. At the railroad station

General Custer told them to go directly to the War Department and wait for him in the Secretary's reception room.

Meanwhile the General went to pick up his wife at the boarding house where she was staying and bring her to witness the ceremony at which he and his spirited cavalrymen were to be honored. But Mrs. Custer was absent, and he spent more than an hour searching for her at the homes of friends.

Elizabeth Custer had hurried to the War Department to meet her husband for the eleven o'clock appointment. He had not yet arrived when the War Secretary came out from his inner office and, introducing himself, invited her to enter. To add to her confusion, promptly on the hour in came the soldiers, each bearing a staff with the flag he had captured.

Secretary Stanton had other scheduled appointments. So he welcomed them all, expressing the nation's gratitude for their deeds at Cedar Creek. Turning to Mrs. Custer, he asked her to respond for her absent husband. She stumbled through a few sentences.

When she had finished, he shook hands with each soldier, asked a few questions of him, and then announced that each was to receive a Medal of Honor and be given a thirty-day furlough. This was a complete surprise to the delighted and proud men.

The brief ceremony had just ended when the breathless and embarrassed General arrived. Taking his hands, Stanton said, "General, a gallant officer always makes gallant soldiers." One of the group shouted, "The 3rd Division wouldn't be worth a cent if it wasn't for him!" and all the men cheered lustily.

Two days later at the White House President Lincoln presented the engraved medals. This was one of the few such occasions, for the Secretary of War usually conferred the honor at the capital city. Most wartime medals were sent to commanders for presentation to the winner in a formal ceremony attended by his entire regiment.

The Chief Executive asked a few questions of each soldier as he placed the medal around his neck. When he came to where Parks was standing at attention ("I was all atremble," he reported), he said to him, "How old are you? You seem much too young to be a hero!"

Trying to keep his voice steady, Jerry replied, "Not quite seventeen, Mr. President," whereupon Lincoln embraced him and whispered with deep emotion, "God bless my boy hero of the Shenandoah."

Jerry Parks always carried the medal with him for the next eight months, until he was discharged with the regiment in July, 1865. He had served sixteen months and was barely over seventeen years old.

He estimated that he had taken part in fifty-five engagements during his term of service. Ever after he was to cherish the memory of his meeting with the dead President and Commander in Chief.

The veteran never returned to his home in northwestern New York. The break with his family had been complete and was never healed. For several years he moved steadily westward. In Illinois both children of his marriage died, and, after a separation, his wife divorced him.

With no family ties whatever, Mr. Parks now satisfied his yearning for life in the rapidly developing West. He was for many years a rancher in Utah, Colorado, and California.

While he was in Colorado in the 1890's, Parks became active in the Colorado National Guard. When the Spanish-American War broke out in 1898, he organized and commanded an artillery battery of Colorado volunteers. The unit was never in action, for the war ended just before its scheduled departure for the Philippines.

In 1927, when he was nearly eighty years old, Mr. Parks died in San Diego, California. He was buried in Arlington National Cemetery.

Jerry Parks' triple capture at Cedar Creek is one of the finest examples of the dash and utter lack of fear exhibited by teenagers in the Union Army.

# CHAPTER 12

## *The Color-Bearer*

LEVY, BENJAMIN B. Musician, Company G, 1st New
York Infantry.

For act of bravery at Glendale, Virginia, 30 June 1862
(when he was seventeen years and four months old).

Citation: "This soldier, a drummer boy, took the gun of
a sick comrade, went into the fight, and when the color
bearers were shot down, carried the colors and saved
them from capture."

Born New York City, 22 February 1845.

Mustered in, 20 October 1861; mustered out, 31 May
1865.

Award made on 1 March 1865.

EACH Union regiment had two flags—the national Stars
and Stripes, with its thirty-four stars (those of the seceded
states were never removed), and the regimental flag. The
latter was more important to the fighting men, for it had
personal significance for them.

Both flags were of the standard dimensions of six and
one half by six feet. Both were carried on a ten-foot staff,
so that they could be seen by all soldiers when held aloft
by the color-bearer.

Civil War battles were fought in accordance with established patterns outlined in printed manuals of military tactics. Charges were made by row upon row of soldiers. When a front row was broken, the ranks were immediately filled up by those in the rear. The flag was the key to the formation of a regiment both in a charge and in an advance to a new position.

"Men, follow your colors!" was the order given by officers as the lines of a regiment moved toward the enemy. All eyes turned to the colors in the forefront, the ranks closed up in files, and a solid, surging front of men advanced. The customary pledge taken by all the members of a regiment when the colors were presented to a newly formed unit was that "It must not be lowered in dishonor, nor polluted by the touch of a traitor."

The capture of the flag by the enemy was looked upon as a disgrace unless the circumstances were extraordinary and clearly unavoidable. Even then a cloud of dishonor hung over the unit, for the loss signified a near or actual defeat.

If the lines wavered or were broken as killed and wounded men fell during a charge, the men would rally and re-form behind the flag, which always indicated the direction of advance.

Each regiment and division (two or more regiments) had two color-bearers guarded by seven soldiers, the color guard, selected for their devotion and coolness under fire. In battle formation the two color-bearers, one holding the national, the other the regimental flag in front of the troops, were flanked by a guard to their left and right. The highest-ranking commanding officer, usually a colonel on foot or mounted on horseback, took his place near them. The first line of soldiers formed six paces behind. Four of the color guard were just behind them, so that they could go to the rescue of an imperiled bearer. A single guard was posted in front of the next line of soldiers.

Through the iron hail of shot and shell the unarmed bearers marched forward with the colors to the line of battle, into the charge, over the earthworks, or against batteries of enemy artillery, closely followed by the first line of soldiers.

To waver for a moment, to break or retreat, even while certain death faced them, would lead to disorganization and possible defeat of the entire regiment. Disaster resulted if the bearers lost their sense of direction. If the colors disappeared for even a minute the soldiers might become confused.

If a regiment broke its lines, retreated, or became panic-stricken, its commander stood by the flag and ordered the soldiers, "Form on the colors!"

Should a color-bearer be shot down, the flag was seized by one of the guard and carried onward in the smoke and din of battle. Should all the members of the guard be killed or wounded, or be far away from the color-bearer, any nearby soldier, officer or private, seized the flag and rallied the men behind it.

More than a tenth of the twelve hundred Civil War Medals of Honor were awarded to color-bearers or soldiers who bore the flags in battle. These included several boys who were in their upper teens.

One of these, Benjamin Levy, was recommended to receive the medal for two acts of bravery involving the flags of his regiment—one for saving both colors in a retreat (for which he was cited), the other for bringing the regimental flag safely back to the lines.

Shortly after President Lincoln's second call for troops and after the disastrous Bull Run defeat, fourteen-year-old Robert Levy enlisted as a private in the 58th New York Volunteer Infantry.

His brother Benjamin, two years older, remained in the New York City home to care for their widowed mother, working at his trade of gilder. Ben's parents had come to the United States from Germany twenty years before, settling in New York. He was born there early in 1845.

Ben's longing to join the army evidently met with his mother's approval. Several of his friends had been in the 1st New York Infantry Regiment since the early days of the war. The regiment was then stationed at Newport News, Virginia, so Ben went there to enlist as drummer of Company G on the twentieth of October, 1861. He then lacked four months of being seventeen years old.

In addition to his duties as drummer, the new soldier became orderly to Brigadier General Joseph Mansfield, whose division was stationed at Camp Butler in Newport News. Ben became a courier carrying dispatches from the General to his superior officer, Major General John Wool, at Fort Monroe.

Fort Monroe was on the north of Hampton Roads, guarding this narrow entrance from the sea into the James River, the water route to Richmond. The south side of the Roads was held by the Confederates, with headquarters at Norfolk. Mansfield's daily messages, which his orderly Levy carried, kept General Wool informed of the activities on the James River.

Levy made regular trips along the northern coast of the Roads in the small army boat *Express,* which left Newport News early each morning, returning from Fort Monroe late on the same afternoon.

The young courier was a passenger on the morning of the twenty-ninth of December. On this trip the *Express* had in tow an old captured prize schooner, the hull of which had been coated with zinc to form a tanker for carrying fresh water. The water was for distribution to the Union vessels on patrol and blockade duty near Fort Monroe.

When the *Express* was in the open water of Hampton Roads at about seven-thirty that morning, the Confederate gunboat *Sea Bird* came out from the opposite side of the Roads and approached. In the gray of the early morning the commander of the *Express* could not at first identify the square flag flying on its signal pole and thought it was a white flag of truce. This was quite natural since Fort Monroe was the principal point for the receipt of Southern mail for dispatch to the Northern states.

But as soon as the *Sea Bird* opened fire he knew that he was wrong. The *Express* put on a heavy head of steam in an attempt to evade capture, for the boat was unarmed and could not return the enemy fire.

The loaded water tank slowed the progress of the *Express,* and the enemy gunboat rapidly gained on her, approaching so close that the gray uniforms of the men on board could be easily distinguished.

On the *Express* young Levy tried to think how he could escape capture and at the same time save the dispatches he carried. They contained information on Union troops which would be valuable to the Confederates.

Suddenly he put his hand in his pocket and felt the new knife he had received a few days before as a Christmas present from his mother. Without asking permission of the officers, he ran to the stern, knelt down so that he would not be a target for the enemy shots, and began to saw away at the hawser which held the water schooner in tow. Because the new blade was razor sharp, he succeeded in cutting the towline quickly, and the schooner drifted away.

Levy then rushed forward to the engineer, told him what he had done, and urged the officer to put on full steam ahead now that the tow load was removed. This he did, heading for the blockading men-of-war lying off Fort Monroe.

The *Sea Bird* came nearer and nearer, setting the *Express* on fire by a shell exploded at short range. But other Union vessels were now approaching, so the enemy gunboat took the water schooner in tow and made for the protection of the Confederate batteries on the opposite shore, returning the brisk fire of the ten vessels now in pursuit. After engaging the shore guns for half an hour, the Union ships abandoned the chase.

Though the tanker had been captured, the *Express* escaped with all on board, and Levy was able to deliver his dispatches safely to General Wool. He was complimented by all on board for his quick thinking, and was commended by both Generals.

Shortly after the *Express* incident, when General McClellan was launching his Peninsular Campaign to advance on Richmond, the 1st New York Volunteers were ordered to leave Newport News. General Mansfield had become attached to his young orderly, and he asked the Colonel of the regiment to allow Levy to remain with him. But the latter pleaded to be permitted to go with his regiment. General Mansfield reluctantly granted his request.

Ben was now back in his old post as drummer, and he drummed through the Peninsular Campaign and in the first five of the Seven Days' Battles. In the retreat (the "change of base" described in Chapter 2) the 1st New York Regiment was on night picket duty and covered the retreat. Confederate guerrillas and sharpshooters lay in wait to capture those who fell behind.

Levy's tentmate was sick with malaria and could not keep up with the others. When it became necessary to leave him behind, Ben smashed his drum and threw it aside, took the equipment and gun of his comrade, and went forward—as a soldier!

On the afternoon of June 30 the regiment took part in the Battle of Glendale, one of several engagements fought that day throughout White Oak Swamp. Being a drummer, Levy was not required to go into this fight. But in spite of this, he boldly marched forward into the battle, eager to do his part.

By the time a retreat was ordered the color-bearers and all the color guard except two had been killed or wounded. The regiment began falling back, and the flags were carried by these two survivors.

Following in the rear, Levy saw one of them drop to the ground, hit by an enemy bullet. He rushed forward and seized the banner from the hands of the wounded man. But just then the other bearer was shot down.

Throwing away the gun that he still carried in one hand, Levy grasped the other colors, and with one staff on each shoulder ran for the safety of his own lines, not stopping for an instant even when he received a flesh wound on the way.

When he came out of the woods with the two flags, Levy found that he was lost. But fortunately he stumbled upon General Philip Kearney, commander of the division which included the 1st New York. The General asked the boy what regiment he belonged to, and even led him to its headquarters.

The young soldier proudly turned over the two flags to the Colonel. For his gallant act he was then and there promoted by General Kearney to color sergeant. Kearney was later to recommend him to receive the medal for this rescue of the two colors, the Stars and Stripes and the regimental flag.

Color Sergeant Benjamin Levy had not even received the written confirmation of his promotion before he was called upon to carry the flag. This was on the very next day, July first, at Malvern Hill, the last of the Seven Days' Battles.

The regiment had been marching since dawn, and the men were so thickly covered with dust that their uniforms looked more gray than blue. While crossing an open field, one of the Union artillery batteries on the hill above opened fire on them, the gunners mistaking them for Confederates.

Seeing the danger, Colonel Dyckman commanded his men to lie down. He then ordered color sergeant Levy, with unfurled flag, to advance down the center of the field and wave the colors until the firing should cease.

Levy promptly obeyed. The artillerymen realized their error, and their firing stopped at once. When he started the return to his regiment, the Confederate sharpshooters concealed near the edge of the woods opened fire on him. One of their bullets hit the flag staff, a second the peak of his cap, and a third the tin cup attached to his haversack.

Ben knew that his dash would be dangerous and make him an easy target. So he lay down while more bullets whizzed over his head. Removing the flag from the staff, he rolled it up. Then he tore his handkerchief into strips and used these pieces to tie the flag into a bundle.

Instead of springing to his feet and running the rest of the distance to the protection of his own lines, young Levy clutched the flag tightly in his arms. Then he rolled over and over until he reached his waiting comrades, who were cheering and applauding him every foot of the way.

Ben carried the colors of the 1st New York in all the other engagements of his regiment. Two months after Malvern Hill he was slightly wounded at Chantilly. When the two-year term of service of the 1st New York expired in May, 1863, Levy was mustered out with Company G.

But he had smelled the smoke of battle too often to be contented with civilian life. Eight months away from army life was all he could bear. So in January, 1864, he re-enlisted, joining a German regiment, the 40th New York Infantry, nicknamed "Mozart," which was on furlough and recruiting replacements.

Though at first a private in Company E, later changed to Company B, Levy's past military experience gained him an early promotion to sergeant. He was almost immediately granted his wish to be under fire again, and fought in battle after battle as a soldier, no longer a drummer, during the early months of the year.

But his continued good fortune was to run out. In the Battle of the Wilderness he was severely wounded, receiving a compound fracture of the left thigh. Unable to move, he lay on the battlefield for many hours before being removed to a field hospital set up in tents.

Most of the wounded there were bedridden and helpless. The next morning the hospital was attacked by Confederate guerrillas who destroyed the tents and drove the wounded men into the open. For two weeks Levy and the others lay on the bare ground with no shelter except the sky for a covering, and with nothing to eat but two hardtack biscuits a day.

Two of the Union doctors and a few soldiers remained with the wounded in the open. One of the male nurses made his way to Fredericksburg, where he reported the situation and location of the little band of unfortunates. Negro troops were immediately dispatched to their relief, bringing them safely to Fredericksburg.

Gangrene was beginning to threaten Ben's leg, and for several months, from July, 1864, until March, 1865, he was in a series of army hospitals, making his way slowly north toward his home in New York City. The physicians in each —at Fredericksburg, at Washington, and at Philadelphia— urged immediate amputation.

But each time Ben begged them to save his leg. Through regular exercise and walking on crutches for seven months, Ben managed to avoid amputation of the leg, though it was shortened several inches.

But when he reached a New York hospital, one of the surgeons reversed the decisions and insisted that the leg must be taken off. Since the wound was on the thigh, this would mean that Levy would be doomed to a future on crutches or with an artificial limb.

When the doctor remained firm in his decision, Levy simply took his crutches one day when the amputation was imminent and limped out of the hospital. He convinced the local army medical authorities that he should be returned to the Washington hospital, where he had had such good care previously.

Ben was finally able to limp without the aid of crutches, and a month before the war came to an end he rejoined his regiment in Virginia for the final campaign.

At that time, on the first of March, 1865, he received his Medal of Honor, forwarded to him from the Washington hospital where it was to have been presented to him by the Secretary of War in person. This Medal was engraved *For gallantry in the Battle of the Wilderness.*

Within a few days, however, a new, corrected Medal arrived, reading *For gallantry at Glendale, Virginia.* This was accompanied by the citation for his carrying of the two colors and saving them from capture.

The error had come about because the various recommendations of six Generals—Mansfield, Kearney, Sickles, Birney, Berry, and Egan—and the Colonels of the two regiments in which he served differed in the specific act they cited.

Benjamin Levy had been nominated for the exploit on the *Express,* for the saving of the two colors at Glendale, for the protection of the regimental flag at Malvern Hill, and for his sufferings in the Wilderness. The Glendale incident was evidently recognized as the most worthy of honor. His regiment is still recorded erroneously as the 40th instead of the 1st New York Infantry in all published lists of Medal of Honor winners.

Sergeant Levy was near Appomattox Court House when Lee surrendered. With his regiment he went to Washington, where he intended to march with his comrades in the grand final review of the Army of the Potomac. Instead, his leg had again become infected and weakened, and he re-entered the hospital, being given a disability discharge the last of May.

After the war, Mr. Levy entered the government civil service and worked as a clerk in the New York Customs House for forty years. A month after his discharge he married "the girl he left behind," and five children were born to them. He died in 1921 at the age of seventy-six.

# CHAPTER 13

## *A Future General*

MacARTHUR, ARTHUR, JR. First Lieutenant and
Adjutant, 24th Wisconsin Infantry.

For act of bravery at Missionary Ridge, Tennessee, 25
November 1863 (when he was eighteen and a half years
old).

Citation: "Seized the colors of his regiment at a critical
moment and planted them on the captured works on the
crest of Missionary Ridge."

Born Springfield, Massachusetts, 1 June 1845.

Mustered in, 4 August 1862; mustered out, 10 June 1865.

Award made on 30 June 1890.

☆　☆　☆

ONE of the most honored general officers in the long history of the United States Army was in his late teens when
he was a soldier during the Civil War. His record of performance and promotions easily matched that of any other
officer in the Union Army.

Though he became known as "the soldier-citizen of the
state of Wisconsin," Arthur MacArthur, Jr., was born near
Springfield, Massachusetts in 1845. His father, Arthur Mac-
Arthur, Sr., who had been born in Scotland, was then practicing law.

When the boy was four years old, the MacArthurs moved

to Milwaukee, Wisconsin. The senior MacArthur was twice elected city attorney, serving four years.

In 1855, MacArthur was elected Lieutenant Governor of Wisconsin. A dispute charging election frauds made him Governor for six days in 1856, but the State Supreme Court, to which the case had been referred, ruled in favor of the opposition. Mr. MacArthur was the innocent victim of political intrigue.

At the beginning of the Civil War he had become Judge of the Second Circuit Court of Wisconsin, a post he held for two six-year terms.

Young Arthur, who had been educated in the city's public schools and by private tutors, lacked two months of being sixteen when the bombardment of Fort Sumter marked the end of any hope for a peaceful solution of North-South differences.

His desire to enlist amounted almost to an obsession. Judge MacArthur argued with his son for hours on end against his becoming a soldier, to no avail. Finally he employed a private guard-tutor to prevent his son from running away. Meanwhile he promised that if Arthur would study military tactics and strategy for a year, until he reached his seventeenth birthday, he would give his consent.

The Judge was never for a moment permitted to forget his promise. As Arthur's seventeenth birthday approached he took action. He decided to use the influence of Wisconsin Governor Edward Salomon to obtain a West Point appointment for his son without any delay.

The Governor wrote a letter of introduction to President Lincoln, and the Judge wrote a personal letter late in May, 1862, in which he said of his son:

...A desire to go into the military service of the country has become an absorbing object of his very existence. This is not a light or sudden impression with him, for he has been dwelling upon it or the Navy for two years so that it has become the fixed bent of his inclination.

... I will add concerning the character of my son that he has a most excellent moral constitution, is free from all personal vices, and gives much intellectual promise.

He closed by offering to send his son to Washington.

President Lincoln evidently granted an interview, for on June third, two days after Arthur's seventeenth birthday, the boy visited the White House with Wisconsin Senator James Doolittle, who was acting as his sponsor.

The Chief Executive immediately determined that the Wisconsin appointments to the United States Military Academy had already been made. The fact that Arthur lacked a year of being eighteen, the minimum age required for entrance, was also unfavorable to the lad's prospects.

Whether or not this disappointing news was broken to Arthur during the interview is not known. The letter of Governor Salomon (now in the U.S. National Archives) bears the written notation of Senator Doolittle: *I introduced young MacArthur to you this morning. He is a splendid youth and his appointment would be among the best.*

The President added a note to his secretary:

I was much impressed with the lad. But no vacancy exists at present. Even if one should occur, I question the wisdom of making an exception to the age rule in his case. This would bring a host of petitioners to my waiting room. Reply, making the blow as soft as possible.

The 24th Wisconsin Infantry Regiment ("The Milwaukee Chamber of Commerce Regiment") was being recruited from Milwaukee and vicinity during the summer of 1862. Arthur volunteered his services as a drillmaster, spending many hours on the parade ground of Camp Sigel, training the recruits. The men finally petitioned Governor Salomon to give him a commission; they honored his skill as a drill-master and admired his personality and his way with them.

Judge MacArthur added a word to the Governor, a not uncommon occurrence at the time. Practically all the top officers of the volunteer state regiments during the war, many of them with no military aptitude or experience whatsoever, were appointed through political influence. Unlike most such appointees, however, Arthur possessed superior military ability in spite of his youth.

So it was that Arthur MacArthur, Jr., was appointed First Lieutenant and Adjutant of the 24th Wisconsin on the fourth of August, when he was seventeen years and two months old.

He was undoubtedly one of the youngest of that rank in the Union Army during the Civil War. He was never even temporarily a Second Lieutenant, nor did he ever serve as a private or noncommissioned officer in either the volunteer or Regular Army.

His first dress parade hardly revealed his potentialities. "Attention, battalion! Shoulder—arms! Prepare to open ranks! To the rear, open order, march! Front!" he ordered in a squeaky voice. Onlookers and the few companies who were able to hear his high-pitched voice grinned openly as the pale-faced stripling marched to the center of the command to finish his duties.

The thousand men of the regiment stifled their laughter as their Adjutant of slim form, awkward gait, and none-too-well-fitting uniform continued issuing orders in his squeaky voice.

The Colonel and other officers were also unimpressed. They resented the boy, whom they said had been "foisted" upon them in the important post.

Governor Salomon supported MacArthur. When the Colonel appealed to him for "a competent man, not a child with an unchanged voice," the Governor sent back word,

"Give the boy a chance." They gave him a chance but were sure he would prove a dismal failure.

When he was told of this complaint, the young Adjutant gritted his teeth and said, "I know why I'm a soldier, and when we get into action I'll do my duty."

The 24th Regiment left Milwaukee during the first week of September, going to Kentucky, where their first battle was at Perryville (Chaplin Hills) in October.

Throughout the fight MacArthur was the only mounted officer the regiment saw or heard. The Colonel was not feeling well and the Major was unfortunately detained elsewhere. The young Adjutant rode along the line, in front of the men, "smiling like a school boy at a snow-balling," and at the right time and in the right place his changing voice rang out with words that cheered the thousand men.

During a lull in the contest, Lieutenant MacArthur rode well to the front to get a look at the enemy. Returning, he hurried along the line and shouted to the men with the same cracked voice that had so greatly amused them two months before, "They are coming, boys! Steady! Hold your fire until they reach the brow of the hill, and then give them a volley." The "boys" did as the boy Adjutant directed. The Confederates were repulsed.

The Colonel (who was deaf!) was evidently humiliated and chagrined, for the next day he resigned, giving poor health as the reason, and left the regiment. "Fell back where nerve-wracking bullets were unheard" was the way the regimental historian put it.

As the 24th Wisconsin Infantry progressed from battle to battle, young MacArthur gained confidence. He had been given his "chance" and had turned out so well that the other officers began to rely more and more upon him for decisions and leadership. He began to be cited in official reports for his invaluable assistance.

He added to his ever growing laurels in the regiment's

second major battle at Stone River (or Murfreesboro), Tennessee, in December. His brigade commander wrote that *he acted with great coolness and presence of mind, ever ready to obey my commands.* The Major commanding the 24th wrote in his official report, *To the Adjutant of the Regiment, Arthur MacArthur, Jr., I am more than indebted for his aid and efficient service rendered during the engagement,* adding, *Young and gallant, I bespeak for him an honorable career.*

Little could he have known at the time how long and honorable it would be!

MacArthur's abilities as a leader and commander were soon tested again in the middle Tennessee and Chickamauga campaigns during the next ten months.

Time and again the men of the 24th Wisconsin were impressed with their Adjutant's fearlessness. With no thought of his own safety, he was always in the forefront of battle. They recognized that he would never ask them to face danger without his presence. Often he seemed oblivious to personal danger.

One of the privates in Company B recounted an incident at the Battle of Chickamauga in September of 1863:

> I was eyewitness to a notably brave deed of the gallant Mac at this battle. When we commenced our retreat, it was discovered that our flag was missing. The color-bearer had the pole, but there was no flag attached. It had been shot from the staff and was hanging on the lower branch of a small oak tree. MacArthur saw it and, spurring his horse toward the rebel lines, he snatched the flag from the oak, amid a perfect hailstorm of bullets, and escaped without injury.

The battles around Chattanooga late in the year were to more than prove his stamina.

It was at the storming of Missionary Ridge that Arthur MacArthur, Jr., still a First Lieutenant, exhibited such fearless and exceptional courage that he became every inch a man instead of a boy. His actions on that day were the beginning of a military career that would eventually raise him to the highest rank in the Regular Army many years later and would win for him the Medal of Honor.

The annals of the Civil War are filled with the names of many large-scale battles equaling in ferocious intensity almost any in American history. Some take their places among the greatest in world history. The daring exhibited by both Union and Confederate soldiers in these furious fights has rarely been surpassed.

The two major battles around Chattanooga, Tennessee, on two successive days in November of 1863—Lookout Mountain (the Battle Above the Clouds) and Missionary Ridge—were perfect examples of encounters in which the performance of the Union Army against seemingly insurmountable odds quickens the pulse a century later.

Chattanooga was a key point for both armies. It was the center of a vital line of communication and supply for Confederate troops advancing northward. It was the key to the Union plan for the movement south into the heart of the Confederacy, Georgia, which was to lead to Sherman's Atlanta campaign and the March to the Sea, splitting the Confederacy in two.

Huge numbers of soldiers and mountains of supplies were dispatched to Chattanooga in September and October following the Southern victory at Chickamauga. This was called the "cracker line." Grant took personal charge of the campaign.

Lookout Mountain, directly to the south of Chattanooga almost on the boundary of Georgia, was the first major encounter. Lookout Mountain drops precipitously several hundred feet above the Tennessee River. The Confederates were posted solidly on the top and around the bottom. A brigade was stationed halfway up the slope.

On the morning of November 24 ten thousand Union soldiers moved against them. After an artillery bombardment on the breastworks and rifle pits along the lower slopes, they charged up the mountain, scaling the rugged heights, cutting their way through felled trees, and driving the Confederates toward the crest.

The struggle on the mountain sides, in dense low-hanging cumulus clouds, which hid the enemy from view, was fierce. While the battle was raging, the cloud on the mountain was so thick that only at intervals could spectators catch a glimpse of the lines and banners. By late afternoon the Union Army was established on the eastern face of the mountain.

Missionary Ridge, immediately to the northeast, was the next target. The Confederate defenses were almost as strong as any during the entire war. Fourteen brigades (twenty-eight regiments) were on the mountain. Another nine were aligned along the base. Three parallel lines of entrenchments—along the base, halfway up the slope, and along the crest—were intended to stop any Union attempt to take the Ridge.

At dawn on the twenty-fifth, the federal attack was ordered. The first attempt was stopped on the lower slopes. The odds against the Yanks were simply too great, the Confederate advantage of terrain and natural position too insurmountable. Between three and four o'clock six cannon shots signaled the assault.

The 24th Wisconsin Regiment was among the many of the Army of the Cumberland to storm up the slopes at that time in the face of galling fire and with complete disregard for their own safety.

The line of battle was almost three miles long. In his memoirs General Grant vividly describes the charge as he viewed it through field glasses atop nearby Lookout Mountain:

Suddenly twenty thousand men rushed forward, moving in line of battle by brigade, with a line of skirmishers in front and closely followed by the reserves in mass. The big siege guns below in the Chattanooga forts roared above the light artillery and musketry in the valley. The enemy's rifle pits were ablaze ... Our men were seen working through the felled trees and other obstructions. Though exposed to such a terrific fire, they neither fell back nor halted, but advanced steadily in a bold and desperate push. The enemy took precipitate flight up the Ridge.

Grant's order had been fully and successfully carried out. The attack had achieved its only purpose—to take pressure off Sherman's forces on the left flank by diversions in the center of the Confederate line. The rifle pits at the foot of the Ridge had been taken, and this in itself was sufficient for the moment.

After a brief halt to re-form the lines, with a sudden impulse all started farther up the Ridge. No order had been given to advance. The idea of storming the heights was too fraught with risk and danger, involving a sure heavy toll in killed and wounded. Such an attack was never even for a moment considered by the top command in planning the strategy.

The men with the muskets and rifles had taken matters into their own hands. In military terminology this is called a "soldier's battle," one "in which the outcome is determined more by the individual courage and initiative of the soldiers and junior officers than by the strategy or leadership of their generals."

Watching this unprecedented movement, Grant turned to his fellow officers and asked each in turn if he had given the order to advance. Each replied, "No, I did not." General Granger, whose corps was making the assault, added, "When those fellows get started, all hell can't stop them." Grant was said to have remarked, "Someone will suffer for it if it turns out badly."

The 24th Wisconsin had made their way nearly a mile across an open plain at the foot of the Ridge under a terrific fire of shot and shell, and had cleared the third line of Confederate rifle pits to the left of the regiments which had already attacked when the unscheduled assault began.

General Sheridan, their division commander, waved his hat and shouted the order, "Go for the top of the Ridge, men!" At least this is what the soldiers later reported. Afterwards the General neither affirmed nor denied that he issued such an order to his division. He may have merely been urging them to seek safety in the captured rifle pits.

They were off! The charge lasted an hour and a half, for every foot of the way presented appalling obstacles. Over two thousand Union soldiers were to be shot down in the assault.

Lieutenant MacArthur was in the advance, urging the men on, "seeming to be everywhere at once." Captain Parsons of Company K described the regiment's part in the assault:

We started up the ascent. Front and enfilading shot from musketry and fifty cannons are plunging down upon us. Some fall, the rest press dauntlessly on. They clamber up the side, hopping ditches, jumping logs, advancing in zigzag lines, rushing over all obstacles, dodging, if they can, the heavy stones thrown upon them by the rebels.

When they were approaching the summit, the color-bearer carrying the regimental flag fell from a gunshot wound. MacArthur seized the colors and carried the flag aloft in front of the regiment, cheering the men to follow him. They passed the second line of breastworks. When they reached the crest and beat back the enemy, MacArthur himself planted the flag in the ground amid the cheers of his men. Of the sixty placed there, that of the 24th was one of the first or second.

A military historian has written that MacArthur was "probably the youngest officer who commanded a regiment under such trying circumstances during the entire Civil War."

The pride of the entire regiment in their Adjutant's exploit was so great that, when the Major in command resigned two months later at the request of General Sheridan, MacArthur, with the consent of all the other officers—the three dozen of the same rank and twelve Captains—was promoted over their heads and made Major. Thus he skipped the rank of Captain, even as earlier he had skipped the rank of Second Lieutenant.

Since he commanded a regiment, even though it was now reduced to a third of its original strength, he was to all intents and purposes a Lieutenant Colonel. He became known throughout the Army of the Cumberland as "the boy Colonel." The displaced Major evidently bore him no malice, for he mentioned MacArthur glowingly in his official report of the battle, the only individual thus cited.

So, when only eighteen and a half, MacArthur was in full command of a regiment, again in all probability the youngest of such rank in the Union Army.

The 24th Wisconsin had by now become a crack regiment, and its subsequent record was an enviable one. After Missionary Ridge, MacArthur and his men moved southward on the slow, hard-fought path to Atlanta from May to September, 1864. The 24th was in every major battle—Dalton, Resaca, Dallas, Kenesaw Mountain, and nine or ten others. MacArthur was always eager to be in the front line.

One day when the regiment was holding a position at Rocky Face Ridge overlooking the Confederate Army around Dalton, Georgia, in May, he was stretched on the ground, resting with one of his officers, who said to him, "Major MacArthur, suppose the rebs down there should make a charge and attempt to get up here, what would you do?"

"I'd fight like hell!" was his quick but quiet reply.

At Jonesboro MacArthur led his regiment in a charge across an open field and forced the enemy from the bordering woods.

At Kenesaw Mountain in June, Major MacArthur was wounded in an attack, but a packet of letters in his breast pocket stopped a bullet aimed at his heart.

After Atlanta had been captured, the 24th was sent north, back to Tennessee. At the Battle of Franklin on the thirtieth of November, MacArthur was credited with saving the day by his superlative command of the 24th Wisconsin Infantry. The regiment arrived after a forced march of twelve miles. By this time, after forty months of continuous service, its strength had dwindled, through dead, wounded, and discharged, from 1,000 to 360 men, making the triumph of Franklin all the more remarkable.

Surrounded by the superior numbers of the enemy, the commander of the Union forces at Franklin warmly welcomed MacArthur, even with his meager number of soldiers.

"Let's get down to business. I am worried," he said. "Please take ten minutes to estimate our situation, then give me a plan to meet it."

The reply was instant. "Sir, I do not need ten minutes. The situation calls for an obvious action. The enemy is closing on us from three sides. I mean to fight like hell."

The commander of the Fourth Army Corps reported on how the 24th Wisconsin fought "like hell":

Our lines had been broken and eight pieces of artillery had fallen into the enemy's hands. At the very moment when the routing of the rebels appeared to be lost and when they were about to turn our own guns on us and retake our batteries, the crisis was at hand.

With an almost fearless spirit, Major MacArthur led his regiment forward to the lost works, took command of the other regiments of the brigade, and restored the battle, retook the eight guns, retook the lost colors of a less fortunate brigade, and captured ten battle flags and four hundred prisoners from the enemy.

He heroically, and to the admiration of his superiors on that occasion, carried on until he was borne from the field disabled by two serious wounds, one in the leg, the other through the breast. He was a model of bravery and manliness, and proved himself one of the outstanding "battle savers" of the War.

The details of the 24th Wisconsin's part in the Battle of Franklin show the regiment's truly magnificent stamina and the high peak of competence which their commander had instilled in them.

On that single day the regiment was in action and under fire for seventeen hours, making repeated charges and assaults, except for two hours of rest from two-thirty to four-thirty in the afternoon. Beginning at four in the morning the soldiers fought until midafternoon without food. They were then ordered to the rear to rest and eat. One of the privates described the interruption of their long-delayed meal:

Our coffee was just beginning to boil and our sowbelly and crackers frying when the rebels charged our breastworks and drove our men out, and followed them up.

They came through our stacked arms and over our fires, upsetting our coffee pots and frying pans, with the rebels right at their heels and at our stacked arms.

Every one of us was as mad as he could be after losing his nearly cooked dinner, and we felt as if we could whip the whole rebel army just at that moment, when Major MacArthur called out, "Fall in, 24th! Take arms! Charge! Give 'em hell, boys. Give 'em hell!"

We did "give 'em hell," and drove them back over the breast-works again.

When the Union troops had been driven back in confusion and MacArthur's order given, the 24th moved to the point of attack, charged with fixed bayonets, retaking the lines which the enemy had just seized. In this charge they fought hand to hand with bayonet and sabre. It was during this action that Major MacArthur was severely wounded.

The regiment held their new position until eleven o'clock at night.

By all reasonable standards, Major MacArthur should long since have been promoted to Lieutenant Colonel. But the small number of soldiers left in the regiment, a little over three hundred, prevented his receiving that honor.

Even the serious wounds received at Franklin left MacArthur undaunted. He was soon back in command, and the regiment fought near Nashville, pursued Confederate General Hood's forces into Alabama, then returned to eastern Tennessee, where it remained until mustered out.

In March, 1865, MacArthur was given a brevet promotion (temporary rank) to Lieutenant Colonel, with two citations "for gallant and meritorious services." One was for the Battles of Perryville, Stone River, Missionary Ridge, and Dandridge. The other was for the Battle of Franklin and the Atlanta campaign.

This was again an almost unique honor, particularly since he was not yet twenty years old. Again, he may have been the youngest Lieutenant Colonel in the Union Army. He was not breveted as a full Colonel until 1868, when he was stationed at Fort Bridger, Washington.

When he was mustered out in June, 1865, MacArthur was just twenty years old, still too young to vote. He had commanded in nine major Civil War actions.

His father was then a judge in Washington, D.C., and his veteran son spent the next year at the family home.

A born soldier, Arthur MacArthur, Jr., joined the Regular Army in May, 1866, becoming Second and First Lieutenant on the same day. Four months later he was promoted to Captain, a rank he was to hold for twenty-three years.

For the next twenty years he was to be stationed in the West fighting Indians. At one time he was aide to General Sheridan, his commander at Missionary Ridge.

Visiting in New Orleans when he was a twenty-nine-year-old officer, he met a girl from Virginia at a ball, and after a six months' courtship by mail they were married in May, 1875. Four of her brothers had fought for the Confederacy, and they refused to attend the wedding.

Two sons were born to them, Arthur III, in 1876, Malcolm two years later (he died when five). In 1880, while he was stationed at the Little Rock, Arkansas, Arsenal, a third son was born. This was Douglas, who was in later years to become even more famous than his father.

Promotions were slow in the Regular Army, and Arthur MacArthur, Jr., was only a Major in 1890 when the Medal of Honor was awarded him. However, in quick succession he became a Lieutenant Colonel, Colonel, Brigadier General, and a Major General (1901).

He served in the Philippines at the turn of the century, then commanded various army departments in the States for the next seven years.

In 1903, while stationed at the Presidio in San Francisco as Commander of the Army Department of California, Major General MacArthur took a month's leave to go to West Point. His son Douglas was to graduate from the United States Military Academy as first in his class. So it was with fatherly pride that he saw his son receive his commission as Second Lieutenant in the Regular Army.

Arthur MacArthur's career reached its high point when, in 1906, he became a Lieutenant General, the highest Army rank at that time. Milwaukee welcomed its foremost soldier-citizen as a resident when he retired in 1909.

The career of General MacArthur, the elder, in both the volunteer and Regular United States Army was so unparalleled that some of its features may well be summarized.

He was not a West Point graduate. He was never a private nor was he a noncommissioned officer. He was never a Second Lieutenant in the Civil War, and bore that rank in the Regular Army for less than a day, in 1866, since his past experience was so impressive that he immediately merited the next highest rank. He was a First Lieutenant during both terms of service, eighteen months during the Civil War, only four months in his Regular Army career. He was not a Captain during the war, passing that rank to become Major of the 24th Wisconsin Infantry. He was, however, a Regular Army Captain for twenty-three years; this was because of the many Civil War officers who joined the Regular Army, making a promotion list of hundreds of names.

For his Civil War service he received seven commissions —two as Colonel, one from the Governor of Wisconsin, the other from the President (a brevet); two as Lieutenant Colonel, one from the Governor, one from the President (a brevet); two as a Major (Wisconsin and U.S. Army); and his first commission as First Lieutenant from Governor Salomon. The state commissions were given according to current custom when the individual Northern states furnished the Volunteer regiments for army service.

In his postwar United States Army service, MacArthur received ten commissions—as Second and First Lieutenant, Captain, Major, Lieutenant Colonel, Brigadier General and Major General of Volunteers (Spanish-American War), Brigadier General and Major General of regulars, and, finally, Lieutenant General, the highest commission given to an officer of the United States Army at that time. It took thirty years to rise from First Lieutenant to Colonel in the Regular Army, though he obtained the same promotions within three years as a Volunteer officer in the Civil War.

Not only was MacArthur one of the youngest Civil War officers, but he was also one of the youngest to hold all ranks. And for much of this time he was in his late teens!

Several decades later General Douglas MacArthur quoted from a British Army song of the First World War: "Old soldiers never die, they only fade away."

His father died surrounded by the old veterans of the regiment he had joined half a century before.

To celebrate the golden anniversary of their regiment's muster in August, 1862, the veterans of the 24th Wisconsin Infantry planned a reunion to be held in Milwaukee on the evening of September the fifth, 1912.

Appropriately enough, the main speaker was to be Lieutenant General Arthur MacArthur, Jr., Retired, who had led them through their entire service during the Civil War.

The heat on that night was oppressive, so much so that the General did not attend the banquet. The air was stifling in the flag-decorated hall in which the meeting was held later after the dinner.

The General began to review the 24th's glorious history from its organization almost exactly fifty years before. Occasionally he pointed out one of his old comrades in the audience. The majority of the hundred-odd men had watched the General's progress from a callow adolescent to a manly, gallant commander.

The atmosphere reflected the closeness peculiar to veterans who have shared army life together. The General had spoken only about ten minutes, when his voice began to waver.

He had brought his listeners in memory through Missionary Ridge and his assumption of full command. As he spoke haltingly of their part in the Battle of Peachtree Creek during the Atlanta campaign, he stopped for a long moment, wiping his forehead.

He had just said, "I am facing the very men I led into that battle..." when he swayed a moment before falling to the floor in a paralytic stroke.

At first those in the hall were frozen with shock. Those nearest him on the platform raised him into a chair and tried to rouse him, but it was useless.

Edwin B. Parsons, ex-Captain of Company K, who had been very close to the General during the many postwar years, suffered a paralytic stroke from the shock of seeing his old comrade fall dead.

The stunned veterans gathered around the easy chair on which he lay and recited the Lord's Prayer together. Someone removed from its staff the regimental flag Lieutenant Arthur MacArthur, Jr., had planted on the crest of Missionary Ridge, and covered his body with it.

His two sons, Douglas and Arthur, went to Milwaukee for the simple, nonmilitary funeral held four days later. The former was then a Captain in the United States Army Corps of Engineers, Arthur a Lieutenant Commander in the United States Navy.

Wordsworth's poem "The Happy Warrior" was read at the service. No better eulogy could have been pronounced than its closing lines:

> This is the Happy Warrior; this is He
> That every Man in arms would wish to be.

The name and traditions of Arthur MacArthur were carried on in the military career of his equally if not more famous son Douglas.

The record of General Douglas MacArthur's honors and

accomplishments would fill many pages. He was one of the youngest Brigadier Generals in army history. Like his father, much of his service was in the Philippine Islands. He came out of retirement to re-enter active service before World War II broke out.

His services then were almost without parallel. He was Commander of the United States Armed Forces in the Far East from 1941 to 1951. He was promoted to General in December, 1941, one of the few five-star Generals during the War. The high point of his service was the stand he made on Bataan Peninsula from December, 1941 to March, 1942, and his later return to the Philippines.

General Douglas MacArthur was soon Supreme Commander of Allied Forces in the Pacific. After the war he was commander of the occupation forces in Japan from 1945 to 1951, and commander of the United Nations forces in Korea until 1951, when he retired.

There was a remarkable similarity in the military careers of father and son. Each served for more than forty-five years. Both advanced through all the Regular Army ranks, and both reached the highest rank possible at the time. Much of the army service of father and son was spent in the Philippine Islands.

But the greatest honor which father and son shared, many years apart, was the award of the Medal of Honor.

The elder MacArthur's medal, awarded when Douglas was a boy a little over ten years old, was for the single Missionary Ridge exploit. His son's, awarded more than half a century later, in April, 1942, was for his leadership in the Philippines from before the beginnings of World War II until he was forced to leave Bataan Peninsula on the twelfth of March, 1942. This was the occasion for his famous statement, "I came through and I *shall* return."

The citation read:

For conspicuous leadership in preparing the Philippine Islands to resist conquest, for gallantry and intrepidity above and beyond the call of duty in action against invading Japanese forces, and for the heroic conduct of defensive and offensive operations on the Bataan Peninsula. He mobilized, trained, and led an army which has received world acclaim for its gallant defense against a tremendous superiority of enemy forces in men and arms. His utter disregard of personal danger under heavy fire and aerial bombardment, his calm judgment in each crisis, inspired his troops, galvanized the spirit of resistance of the Filipino people, and confirmed the faith of the American people in their armed forces.

This high award came after General Douglas MacArthur had been twice recommended previously. The first was for action in Vera Cruz, Mexico, in 1915, but at that time war had not been declared, so the nomination was rejected.

The second nomination was for his services as a Brigadier General in France during World War I. The war had just ended, and it was decided not to make the award to any general officer.

Arthur MacArthur, Jr., and his son Douglas are the only father and son to have been awarded the Medal of Honor throughout its century-old history.

It must not be forgotten that the award of the Medal of Honor is the highest recognition which a grateful nation can bestow upon a soldier, whether he is a private in the ranks, a noncommissioned officer, an officer, or a five-star General.